BACKPACKING
A Hedonist's Guide

If you can't find a Moon Publications title
in your local bookstore, ask them to place
an order through:

Moon Publications, P.O. Box 1696, Chico CA 95927
  tel. (916) 345-5473 / 345-5413

Bookpeople, 2929 Fifth St., Berkeley, CA 94710, tel. (415) 549-3030
  toll free orders: (800) 642-4466 in California; (800) 227-1516 in continental U.S.

Publishers Group West, 5855 Beaudry St., Emeryville, CA 94608
  tel. (415) 658-3453

BACKPACKING
A Hedonist's Guide

BY RICK GREENSPAN & HAL KAHN
ILLUSTRATIONS BY GORDON OHLIGER

moon
PUBLICATIONS

Library of Congress Cataloging in Publication Data

Greenspan, Rick.
  Backpacking : a hedonist's guide.

  Bibliography: p.
  Includes index
  1. Backpacking--United States. 2. Outdoor
cookery. I. Kahn, Hal, 1930- . II. Title.
GV199.4.G74 1985   796.5'1   85-2939
ISBN 0-918373-00-X

BACKPACKING: A HEDONIST'S GUIDE

Published by
  Moon Publications
  P.O. Box 1696
  Chico, California 95927

Cover Design by
  Gordon Ohliger

Printed by
  Colorcraft Ltd., Hong Kong

CONTENTS

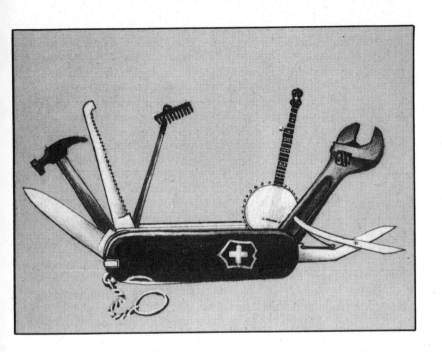

INTRODUCTION

Brooklyn Boy Meets Wilderness

Steve looks like a surfer but sounds like a mobster. Behind the Dayglo tan and obedient muscles is a bookish film critic from Flatbush who'd never been closer to the wilderness than summer camp at Bear Mountain. The Great Outdoors ("outta daws") meant Belmont Racetrack and Shea Stadium. The only trails he'd ever hiked were asphalt.

But like many young city slickers, he craved the country. We'd never taken anyone backpacking who was so eager to "tame" the wilderness. He couldn't wait to strap on the pack and get started. He was strong and fit. He was ready for bear! He lasted about 3 hours. Several miles from the trailhead, he began to mutter and grumble. Howinhell could anyone enjoy schlepping a 40-pound pack uphill in 80 degree heat all afternoon toward some abstract promise of a cool mountain lake? The farther we got from the last beer, the darker became his mood. His shined boots were a size too small; long before our destination they had rubbed his heels raw. His pack felt like some mythic burden of the damned. The route was incomprehensible. By the time we stopped for dinner, he was ready for a hotel. But a quarter-inch foam sleeping pad was not his idea of the Waldorf-Astoria.

The second day brought no relief. Up too early, we climbed 1,500 feet in the first mile, then set off cross country around a mountain bowl strewn with rock slides, boulders and steep pitches into space. The streets of Brooklyn seemed safe by comparison. Steve's every muscle ached from yesterday. We kept up a steady stream of encouragement, however, and by mid-afternoon, Steve made a monumental discovery. You can make the pack work *for* you, keeping the weight on the hips and off the shoulders. He began to notice that the view before him was improbably remote and beautiful, something he couldn't see elsewhere. And when we finally climbed down to a granite-girded lake, filled with trout and inaccessible enough to promise a week of solitude, Steve remembered why we came: 7 days of fishing, cooking, eating and relaxing.

His contentment lasted till we set out to catch our supper. Steve regarded the fishing rod with suspicion. We put a lure on the line and taught him how to cast, but that did nothing to dispel his skepticism. How could you catch fish with a spoon-shaped piece of metal at the end of a line? He cast and cast—aspersions and oaths as well as lures and flies and bubbles. Around the lake he went. No luck. He announced his early retirement from the game.

His mood blackened as the clouds rolled in, necessitating another trauma—setting up his tent. He hesitated. We cajoled. He procrastinated. We insisted. He refused. We quickly erected it. It began to pour. It rained all night. In the morning, Steve's tent looked like a collapsed dream the day the circus leaves town. Somewhere under that heap of netting, nylon and wind-sundered rainfly lay a sodden backpacker converted to the virtues of foul weather protection. While the sun dried his sleeping bag, Steve spent an hour erecting the tent in the ideal place with geometric fanaticism. It looked great, and he never spent another moment in it. But he was glad it was there, waiting.

The next day Steve caught his first fish, an 8-inch brown trout, with a grasshopper. Well, perhaps he'd consider coming out of retirement. Two days later he returned with 7 little rainbows after a tough solo hike to a lake beyond the razor-back ridge. And he began to *talk* fishing. He studied the "hatch" of flies on the water's surface, invented fishing knots, and experimented with salmon eggs as extra enticement on his lures. Trout with almonds, trout baked in soy sauce, ginger and garlic, fish grilled over red hot coals at sunset—all helped make the talk better. Backpacking began to look—and feel—like fun.

On our fifth day, Steve set out to bake a cake. He'd never before baked anything, anywhere. He had, however, been impressed with the cinnamon nut bread and the chocolate cake with icing we'd pulled from the coals. He hauled out flour and baking powder, corn meal (which he mistook for milk powder), RyKrisp, raisins, apricots and sugar; mixed them all in a pot; added some margarine, sugar, an egg, then poured in just enough water to make the batter run off the spoon like a ribbon. We reminded him to grease the pot before surrounding it with hot coals, wished him luck and went fishing. When we returned an apricot cornbread awaited us. And Steve carved another notch on the stock of his backpacking knowledge.

After that, we had a wilderness fanatic on our hands. He insisted on doing everything: fishing, sewing, cooking, gathering wood. We managed to keep busy swimming, sunning, eating and reading. Together we invented ways to cook fish, fry corn cakes, and coined new names for the constellations in the night sky because we weren't sure of their classic names and didn't care. By the time we walked out, Steve was a confirmed backpacker, and we were convinced that anyone could become one too.

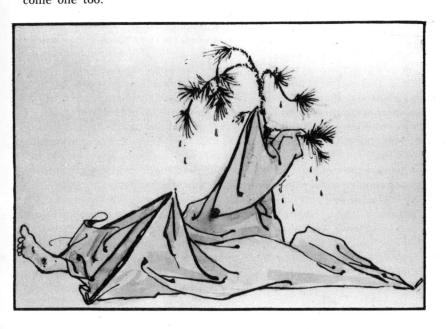

What This Book Is About

There are enough texts on hiking, backpacking, car camping, mountaineering, survival and fishing to fill a four-year curriculum on the fine art of leaving your house. This book doesn't duplicate the other guides. Rather, it illustrates just how a 7 to 9 day wilderness trip works.

We recognize the long and honored tradition of hiking for the sake of hiking—of covering ground. But this book is based on a different idea: that a remote lake, surrounded by mountains, filled with trout and warmed by sunshine is its own attraction, a place that is ideal to settle into for a week or more. If you're a novice, we want to show you three things: how to determine where to go; how to get there; what to do there. If you're an old hand at backpacking, we'll give you different information: about fishing, cooking, trail-finding and stargazing.

A book can't catch a fish or bake a cake. It *can*, however, provide the initial inspiration, point in the right direction and mainly, cut the time, cost and hard knocks of learning. We'll show you how to stay dry, stay full, stay busy, stay friends. We'll run you through the basics— equipment, packing, maps, trails—and then give you hints on improvising: making souffles, fishing in the rain, repairing boots, naming constellations. We want to give you a feel for the limitless possibilities of a backpacking trip.

We do make several assumptions: that you like to camp and love to eat; that you want a vacation, not a forced march; that you're eager to escape the madding crowd. We also assume that you are not necessarily a mountain climber, spelunker, trail blazer, Yukon guide or even a Sierra Club member. You may never have set foot on a wilderness trail or you may have walked them for years. You are reasonably fit but not a triathlete. You believe that locomotion by foot is an honorable and even enjoyable way to travel, and that a wilderness trip does not require a seat on the New York Stock Exchange to finance it.

One of us is afraid of heights, but gets along fine even on steep trails. We've been lost and even without radar have managed to figure out where we were and how to get to where we were going. We don't have the newest, most expensive equipment. But we've lived on fish we caught, baked breads and cakes, read some of the world's longest novels, kept our clothes dry and spirits up in 48 hours of steady rain, and come back to spin tales that make our friends' feet itch and our own thoughts turn to the next trip out. Everything we write about we've done ourselves, and most of it we learned by doing. All the stories are true. And if we haven't done something—for example, coped with serious injury—we don't write about it. We prefer to go easy on detailed information you can get better elsewhere. (We do, however, suggest where to get this information. See ''Appendix.'')

How To Use This Book

We've never met anyone who has actually read a backpacking book cover to cover. You'll probably want to cut in at functional points, then cut out. To that end, we divide the book into 3 parts: PLANNING A TRIP, GETTING THERE, and BEING THERE. Here's a brief summary of each:

Planning A Trip

Planning a backpacking trip is hard work. It takes a lot of time and energy. It requires making lists, checking them twice. It requires deciding where, when, with whom to go, and how to get there. Then you must assemble gear, maps, permits, more gear. In Chapter 1, we show you how to plan trips for one person, 2, 4, or more, for families and extended families—bringing babies and great-grandmothers takes only a little special forethought. We also suggest ways of choosing where to go—from hiking guides to word-of-mouth information. Chapter 2 is all about equipment—with a twist. We show you how to stay warm, dry and comfortable, *without spending a fortune*. Chapter 3 concerns food: what and how much to take, where to buy it, how to weigh and pack it, what utensils, stoves and pots you'll need, even how to cache food on a long trip. After this planning is done, cooking and eating is a piece of cake! In short, it will take an hour to absorb these suggestions and 3 or 4 days to plan your trip. But we guarantee to save you countless hours and dollars and hassles.

Getting There

You've planned and prepared your backpacking adventure for a week. You've got everything. You're at the trailhead. Chapter 4 takes you on to your destination. It shows how to obtain and read maps, load and adjust a pack, hike a trail and negotiate off-trail terrain. It tells what to eat and drink while hiking which, as you'll see in the cooking chapter, is far different from your diet while in camp. We suggest how to decide how far to go in a day. But above all, we stress the importance of remaining flexible. A blister, storm, headache or meadow full of wildflowers may slow you down or change your plans. This is a vacation. Look around, enjoy, take it easy.

Being There

You've hiked for 2 days into the backcountry. You've just reached your campsite, either the intended destination or an inspired discovery. In our camping chapter (5) you'll find suggestions on setting up a campsite and keeping yourself and the environment clean. You'll get a feel for filling those long summer days with pleasure: reading, mending, climbing, identifying flora and fauna, collecting firewood, playing cards, making love, staring at the scenery.

Above all we like to fish and eat. This is the meat of the book. In Chapter 6 we show you backcountry techniques for catching wise and wary fish without the latest in laminated fly rods. A purist might cringe, but we've never gone hungry. And neither will you.

If you've never boiled an egg you can still bake a trout souffle. The cooking chapter (7) shows how to become a wilderness chef without burning yourself, the food or the forest. Our attitude toward food lies somewhere between the Spartan commitment to nuts and berries and the Epicurean insistence on steak and potatoes. If you enjoy eating in your own kitchen, why deprive yourself of the pleasure just because you're 3 days and 9,000 feet away from a home with a range? Stick with us and you can have your backcountry cake and eat it too!

Nighttime entertainment is usually limited to poking the embers of a dying fire, exchanging tales, keeping warm and watching the stars. We've tried in our star chapter (8) to give you a couple of working methods for making *personal* sense out of the slice of sky above you; it's legitimate to see constellations with your own mind's eye. Just as ancient Greeks and Chinese discovered different formations in the same stars, you may rearrange the classical sky for yourself with much pleasure and no damage to the astronomical establishment. If you're a traditionalist and want to know how to read a star map, the information is here. You'll never know how bright the night sky is until you see it unadorned by city lights or free of a cover of smog.

Note To Readers

The best wilderness guidebooks have pages missing. Somebody has spotted a hint too good to forget, lifted the information and stowed it in the pack along with the maps and cookies. That's how to treat this

—

book. Tear away. Stuff the fishing info in the plastic bag you'll use for a tackle box; file the recipes with the toilet paper; wrap extra flashlight batteries in the star guide. By the time you've used the hoary wisdom contained in these pages, you'll no longer need it. Three loaves of mountain bread and a baked trout into the trip, you'll be on your own. The information will have become food for thought and the pages will then be ready to become fuel for your fire. If things work out the way we think they will, your innovations will be better than ours, and if you don't mind sharing them they'll become part of the bigger, better-than-ever, completely revised and lavishly illustrated second edition.

Acknowledgements

The people who made this book possible are the ones who've traveled with us, sharing our pleasure in wilderness backpacking and helping us test the depths of our ability to improvise and have fun. They are all in the book, mostly under their own names, though sometimes shaded by a "moniker." To them our thanks has often been spoken privately; here it is made public, and we hope they enjoy reading the words as much as we enjoyed writing them.

Karen Bernstein and Deke Castleman can recite the entire text of the book by heart. That's because they've read it so many times, as two of the world's all-time tough and compassionate editors. If you want bear stories and highfalutin' backpacking philosophy, you'll find them on the cutting room floor, victims of a conspiracy against Fluff and Solemnity.

Rob Kessler, Doug Murray and Sharon Pastori, all expert backpackers, read an early version of the manuscript and so changed it with their suggestions that the final product is theirs too. Finally, all those anonymous trail crews, rangers and strangers we've met in the mountains deserve a nod and a note of thanks as well. There is a great store of friendship in the backcountry, and we seem to have drawn on it more than most. Our book is a little gesture of repayment, and we hope our friends take it as that.

PART ONE:
Planning A Trip

CHAPTER I:
Getting Ready

Crystal Lake

"It was like looking into a fishbowl. The water was crystal clear and the fish must have been 2 feet long." Rick's friend Alice described the high country lake she had visited as a child, over 10 years ago. "Half a dozen adults, 4 kids and our guide, Big Buck, traveled by horseback for 3 days, stopping each night at a different lake. On the fourth day, we left the horses, and hiked up a steep ridge, down a gravelly streambed, across several mountain ridges and snowfields, and down a boulder-strewn gully to Big Buck's favorite lake.

"This was our destination. It lay nestled between a pine forest and a snowfield, in a basin outlined by sheer granite walls. It was fed by bubbling brooks and waterfalls. The water was clear, the fish huge. I'll never forget it. It was called Crystal Lake.''

Alice never returned; one magical trip had been enough. Besides, without Big Buck as a guide, how could it be done? But Rick was intrigued. He gathered maps and guidebooks, checked indexes and keys, and finally found it: Alices's recollection was remarkably accurate. The route was easy to spot, and the maps showed him locations nearby for a sheltered campsite with fresh water. Looking closely he found a different route back, over more difficult terrain, but passing another isolated lake. He set off alone in late September.

Using maps, compass, planning and common sense, he left the trail high in the mountains, crossed several miles of rocky, rough terrain and arrived. Superb weather, gorgeous views, a secure campsite and incomparable fishing assured the kind of trip that even Alice in her particular wonderland could not have imagined. Rick's trip to Crystal Lake gave him a new confidence about backpacking. The wilderness beyond the trail was no longer a mystery and Big Buck's route to a high mountain lake was not magic anymore.

Where To Go

One way to choose a backpacking destination is through a book or magazine. Libraries, book and camping stores offer trail guides and commentaries. Local newspapers, newsletters and magazines often describe campsites and trails. (We've listed some suggestions in our "Appendix," but the farther you are from California, the more you'll have to hunt up sources on your own.) Be careful to notice the difference in difficulty between hikes for beginners and those for experts. Don't start toward a scenic wonderland, only to discover you overlooked the section that mentioned the roaring river you'd have to ford.

The best way to find a destination for a week-long backpacking trip, however, is by word of mouth. Ask your friends. Ask their friends. Check with salespeople at the outdoor sports supply store, contact local photographers, ask old-timers. Contact the Sierra Club, local wilderness groups, the Boy Scouts. Check with resort owners, guides, camp counselors.

Know in advance how far you want to drive, and hike. Do you need a trail? Expect to catch fish? Then you hit up the experts with, ''We're looking for a place about four hours' drive away, for a four or five day outing, with really good fishing.'' The precision of the answers will be determined by the precision of the questions. Don't worry if the answers are vague. Don't limit yourself to one or 2 suggestions. There are advantages and disadvantages to any spot. Keep checking out people, places and possibilities. Collect secret spots like CIA agents collect microfilm.

Then locate the spots on a map. If you can't find them on paper, there's no sense hiking out into the wilderness to look for them. Figure distance, elevation and hiking difficulty by studying the maps (see Chapter 4 for where to get maps and how to read them). With a little practice, this is easier than you think. Once you've figured out where to go, start thinking about how long and how far.

How Far Can You Go?

It's one thing to leave the wilderness feeling exercised and healthy; it's quite another to limp out with blisters and sore muscles. A slow pace starts you off, so to speak, on the right foot.

A weekend trip is the most difficult to plan if you want to get away from it all without killing yourself in the process. If you take off after work on a Friday, drive a couple hours to a trailhead, and start out bright and early Saturday morning, don't plan on hiking more than 2 or 3 miles. Scenic lakes close to the trailhead are apt to be crowded; we suggest you stick to a river or stream, stake out an isolated campsite, then relax Saturday afternoon and Sunday morning before hiking out.

A 3 or 4 day weekend is a bit easier to accomplish, though beware of long holiday weekends. It's much harder to avoid crowds over 4th of July weekend than the one before or after. However, this book is primarily concerned with a full week in the wilderness. That allows you to drive longer, and hike farther into the mountains.

The Drive

We often drive a whole day to get to the trailhead (the place you leave your car). Usually, you can sleep there the night before you begin hiking. But it's often hard to sleep that first night if you're excited about the trip, tired from work and running around getting ready. So you may start your first full day of hiking with less than optimum energy.

Sunday Hike

If you arrive on Saturday, you'll usually start hiking on Sunday. Even if you don't sleep too well, a night at the trailhead helps acclimate your body to the altitude. Still, you're in the mountains, between 6,000 and 10,000 feet. You head uphill with a heavy pack. High elevation means less oxygen per lungful; it also means possible altitude sickness. The first day is not one to push yourself.

Most people can cover 3 to 5 miles uphill the first day without undue strain, usually at a rate of about 45 minutes per mile—about 4 hours total. More than 5 miles uphill tends to cause leg cramps and sore feet; it can also drive you to despair that you're working so damned hard on your vacation. If you start at the crack of dawn, as we strongly recommend, take a candy-bar break after a mile and another at about 3 miles. You'll reach your destination in early afternoon, ready for lunch and a swim.

Second Day Hiking

Figure on covering more ground than you did the day before. When you stop Monday afternoon, you're approximately 10-12 miles from the trailhead. The weekend hikers are gone. You're probably alone at a pretty mountain lake or streamside.

The Payoff

Day number 3 might be pure relaxation: catch some trout, read, explore, lie in the sun. Especially if you're by yourselves, you can get the peace and quiet you were searching for. You might move camp in the next several days, to a lake even further from the beaten path. Then again, you might not.

Getting Home

Six days into the trip will find you ready to stay for a month but having to think about getting home. If you've hunkered down at that day 3 campsite, it won't be far back to the trailhead, and you can do the whole return trip on the 7th day. If you've gone farther off or down the trail, you might start back on the 6th day, make a quick camp that evening and head out early in the morning. In any case, most of the food will have been consumed, the packs will be light, and it'll be mostly downhill walking. Who cares how tired you'll be when you get to the car? Adrenaline and fond memories will keep you awake on the freeway. Before cranking up the engine, check the water, oil, and tires. And be sure to do a quick last check to determine that you haven't left the tent or the borrowed pack lying in the dust before driving off.

Rules Of Thumb

Here are some general rules that we use to plan our trips:

- A morning of hiking deserves an afternoon of rest.
- A full day of hiking deserves a full day of rest.
- On the first day of a trip, no more than 5 miles in distance and 1,500 feet in elevation.
- On succeeding hiking days, no more than 7 miles in distance and 2,000 vertical feet.

How Many Are Going?

There are no rules about the number of people that can go on a trip, but you should have some idea what the different numbers mean. Going alone is a lot different from going with one other person, or with 2 or 20. We once met a party of 15 far off the trail in the Sierra wilderness who seemed content and happy. We never figured out how such a large group could hold together and we shudder at the thought of having to organize such an expedition. But clearly it can be done. However, if the object is to recapture a bit of solitude and to relax, keep your forces down. We've traveled alone, as a pair, in a threesome, with 4 and with 6.

Soloing

Solo backpacking is a special and satisfying art, though going one-on-one with nature has its own requirements. A week is a long time to spend by yourself. And while being alone is not the same as being lonely, it does call for a good set of inner resources in top working order. Keeping busy isn't hard. But since the kind of trip we're describing isn't a 20-mile-a-day grind, if you don't like tinkering with fishing lures, devising new ways to cook trout, reading, or just sitting, you may get antsy. That's OK, you've got plenty of room for restlessness and plenty of space to pace. In solo backpacking, all your emotions become more intense: the questions, worries, phobias, as well as the rewards, highs and joys. Also, you alone get to make and unmake all the plans. And the only problem you'll have with "human dynamics" is figuring out how to get along with yourself.

If you do solo, you'll have to sacrifice some weight that would otherwise be shared. The inflatable raft you might want for those lazy days on the lake will stay behind. The extra cooking pot, set of lures, roll of film, cinnamon container, may drop out as well. But for almost everything you leave behind, you can improvise with what you've got. You can make a raft, roast fish in the coals, sketch instead of taking pictures, fashion lures with your hooks, or substitute flaked chocolate for cinnamon.

The more experience you have backpacking with others, the better equipped you'll be to go it alone. The same is true of solo backpacking off the trail: experience *in a group* is a prerequisite. Any kind of hiking is safer, more fun and more confidence-building when done at first with others.

With Others

But how many others? First, it's useful to understand that backpacking is not a personality-altering exercise. For all the solace and rejuvenation your trip provides, you're apt to take in and bring out the same likes, dislikes, habits and concerns that you carry around every day. The same is true of your friends. What pleases you or irks you about them will tag along, and may well be heightened by the strange environment.

The more people there are, the harder it is to achieve compatibility, the more time and patience necessary to make the trip work well for everybody. With larger groups, decision-making takes longer, and is more emotionally draining. There are more ideas and opinions to deal with. Complications increase exponentially. A 6-person trip is not 3 times as complex as a 2-person trip: it's 9 times.

Try to straighten things out as much as possible beforehand. Talk over what you each like to do and eat, and what you can't stand. Discuss relative experience, physical fitness, allergies and ailments. Figure out who knows what. Share any information you can. The expert who makes you feel like a fool is dispensable; leave him or her home. The one who makes *you* feel like an expert is, at 9,000 feet, the most wonderful human being on earth.

There are other advantages and disadvantages to numbers. The more people, the more you can bring — an extra book, chocolate bars, a shovel. Tasks can be shared and loads lightened. On the other hand, some lakes you want to camp at have only one small campsite, barely room for two. And the bigger the party, the harder it'll be to concentrate on the sounds of silence.

If a very young (even a baby) or a very old person is going along, special arrangements for sharing loads and responsibilities need to be worked out beforehand. *Really* worked out. Otherwise one or 2 people will end up harassed, overworked, and unhappy. Count animals in your calculations, too. Dogs are wonderful companions in the wilderness and can carry their own food on the trail, but off-trail you must carry it for them—the probability of their tearing a pack on rough terrain and losing the food is high. And remember, unless you have a Siberian husky, Malamute or some other pooch who is happiest in inclement weather, you'll share limited tent space with wet fur on those rainy nights. But as long as the trail is not too rocky for their footpads or off-limits to pets (as in National Parks), they're great to have along.

Regardless of the number of people and pets, there are several useful rules to go by:

• The slowest person sets the pace. Plan distances for the day or week with this in mind. If you have to stop short of those goals, well—it just doesn't matter. This is particularly important with children. It once took Hal 2 days to hike 2 miles with his children (ages 7 and 10) on their first backpacking trip. Even then it was harder for them than he'd expected. But the slow pace was right and they still reminisce about the marmots, snow cones, small brown trout and, yes, the tough climb and heavy packs.

• Stay together. This is particularly important if you're going off the trail ("cross country"). If there are 4 of you, you can go in pairs, but even then all 4 should follow the same route. Most serious accidents occur when one person hikes alone.

• Cater to individual needs. If someone hates to cook, don't make them feel they must. This isn't a test, it's a vacation. If someone doesn't know how to cook but wants to, help them out, but let them do it. This isn't a three-star French restaurant, and if the bread burns or the fish falls in the fire, so what? You'll still eat and you'll go back with a funny story.

• Share leadership and decision-making as much as possible. Let everyone take the lead on the trail. This is a matter of courtesy, and it's important. Many guidebooks suggest appointing a leader, someone who knows in advance he or she will have the final say in any difficult decision. This is good advice in emergency situations. The person with the most experience might be best to lead you up a mountainside or across a snowfield, but in most cases, there doesn't need to be much structure. Most decisions are better made by consulting everyone and finding a common denominator. Flexibility is the key: stay loose and happy.

CHAPTER II:
What To Bring

Danger! Big Bucks

Those faded photographs of the early backpackers like John Muir and his pals are probably banned in better camping stores. There's not enough equipment in them: no aluminum frame wraparound packs, self-standing dome tents, color coordinated climber's shorts, not even sleeping bags. Just wood and wool. In those days, goose down was still the underside of Christmas dinner. Nylon and Gortex were not even gleams in an inventor's eye. Nevertheless, those pioneer trekkers were well prepared and equipped. They just weren't fashionable.

We don't subscribe to "old is beautiful" or "back to basics" nostalgia. The new lightweight equipment is extremely valuable. But that doesn't mean you have to go broke using it. Backpacking has become big business, and it's easy for ads and sales pressure to convince you to buy a lot of costly equipment before you can safely, comfortably or competently hit the trail.

The way out of this financial bind, we call "functional shabbiness," with the emphasis on functional. Hal is a classic practitioner. He began hiking in work boots, which he repaired at every campsite. After they fell apart on the trail, he bought a pair of irregular hiking boots on sale at a factory outlet, and has worn them ever since. He used a Taiwan-made sleeping bag for 8 years until there was no loft left, then got a Polar Guard bag. He's never owned a backpack, preferring to borrow a 12-year old model with a re-welded frame, so disreputable that a shoe store, asked to replace a pouch zipper, refused to work on it. Hal isn't very pretty on the trail, but he does keep safe and solvent.

Like most people you don't have a lot of money to spare, but you can manage by scavenging, improvising, borrowing and renting. An old shower curtain can become a tarp or tent; a padded book mailer can serve as a camera case. You'd be surprised at the number of ways to re-cycle plastic, wire or bits of material into functional backpacking neces-sities. Rick, for example, developed a list of 47 functions for a bandana with a safety pin! And the more familiar you become with the routines and rhythms of backpacking, the more inventive you'll be.

If you plan to borrow, some rules should be followed carefully. Make an accurate list of everything you need to borrow. Then make duplicate lists of everything you *do* borrow. Keep one and leave the other with each lender. Make sure you both agree on its contents. Check the condition of the borrowed gear with the lender. Know what shape it's in before you use it. Return all items clean. Replace and re-pair (or have repaired) every piece of lost or damaged equiment, even if the damage is minute or superficial. Don't assume that the owner won't notice a missing strap, torn parka, clogged fuel vent or half-empty Band-Aid box. Finally, make a voluntary cash contribution to the lender when you return the equipment. This is both a gesture of thanks, and a way to let the lender add a little something to the equip-ment stash. Gear is expensive, and anyone who lends it to you is a real friend. If you use care and consideration, you'll maintain the friend-ship and be able to borrow again.

Renting equipment is useful for testing items you're considering buying, or for things you use infrequently. Renting also makes sense if you aren't sure how much you'll like backpacking in the first place, or if 7 avid first-timers show up on your doorstep ready to head into the

Great Void with nary a kerchief to their names. Many camping and recreational stores have rental services where it's now possible to get almost everything you need for a trip.

If you have some money to invest, it's worthwhile to buy equipment which will last. Plan to assemble a set of decent equipment over several years. Shop slowly and carefully. Get advice from friends, experts and sales people. Also, study the semi-annual catalogues of the great camping and mountaineering stores such as L.L. Bean and Recreational Equipment, Inc. (R.E.I.). Their information is reliable, fastidious and based on expert experience and testing. Their prices are competitive and fair (see "Appendix" for catalogue addresses). Remember to bargain!

Sandwich Of Warmth

Clothing

In assembling clothing, try to use what you've got with an eye to traveling light and staying warm and dry. Within those requirements tastes will vary. Some people are cool and comfortable in shorts; some hate having their bare legs covered with dust and sweat. Some women swear by halter tops, others by T-shirts to keep pack straps from chafing. Hats and underwear are as much articles of faith as clothing:"To wear or not to wear?" is thus a religious question. Follow your conscience.

Our English friend Claire began her first backpacking trip in white shorts. Five minutes after we hit the trail, they were no longer white. And eight days later, they were ready for the dumpster. Another friend discovered after 4 days that his 3 ragged woolen sweatshirts were too heavy to carry and unnecessary for summer weather. He burned them one afternoon while baking bread, along with his "spare" hiking boots.

The minimum kit goes something like this: 2 T-shirts, a warm shirt, sweater or sweatshirt, a pair of jeans, a pair of long-johns or light pants (sleepwear on cold nights), a pair of shorts, as much or little underwear as you like, 3 pair of heavy socks, a warm jacket (down or fiber-filled are lightest), a wool hat, sun visor, and rain poncho that can double as a ground cloth. We'll discuss boots below. If everything fits in a normal sleeping-bag-sized stuff sack which weighs no more than 12 pounds, you're in business.

There are several extras that we always take along: a pair of gloves for warmth, wood gathering and pot holding; a bandana for the brow, nose, and neck; a pair of light-weight moccasins, old sneakers or thongs for the campsite (and crossing streams); extra poncho(s) in order to fish in the rain without taking the groundcloth out from under the tent; and a towel. Remember that even damp towels are heavy. Take only one and share it.

After that you're on your own. If something gives you particular pleasure—a wash cloth or a party hat, a tallis or a cummerbund—take it. A couple years ago, we were startled to see, across a wilderness lake, a woman standing on a rock, dressed in a full karate outfit with a *kendo* stick in hand. Colored by the setting sun, she was an unexpected and picturesque sight. Her whim had cost extra weight, but was worth it in charm, and, we suppose, in self-satisfaction.

layering: Layering is a truism in backpacking. Early in the morning and at night, you'll probably wear almost everything you've brought. But what if you're still cold? In camp, sit by the fire, huddle next to someone, or get into your sleeping bag with your clothes on, with someone else, if necessary. If all else fails, borrow from a friend who may be better insulated. On the trail, it's rarely a problem: after a quarter-hour or so, you'll be so warm you'll shed clothes, not add them. In fact, it's important to shed layers before your sweat makes the inner ones damp.

Layering becomes a problem if your clothes are wet from sweat or rain. If your T-shirt gets sweaty, change it. The same goes for wet socks—which make your feet hotter and hotter. In fact, they'll burn, causing blisters and soreness. So always wear socks that are both clean and dry. Take 3 pair. You can wash one (which will dry suspended from the pack as you hike), wear one and keep one in reserve. Some people like light cotton socks next to the skin and heavy wool hiking socks over them. Cotton absorbs sweat and keeps the outer sock dry.

If it starts raining on the trail, make sure that both you and your clothes' sack are protected by a poncho, plastic garbage bag, tree, anything. If you fall in a river, take time to dry your clothing or hang it from your pack as you hike. If you're sleeping in the open, keep tomorrow's clothes in your sleeping bag, or in a stuff sack which can double as a pillow. It's not exactly wash'n'wear, but remember that a combination of wet, cold and wind can cause hypothermia (lowered body temperature), which can be fatal, and is the backpacker's nightmare. Take all precautions against it. (See Chapter 4, under "Hiking in the Rain.")

keeping clean: One year, 4 of us were climbing down a steep bowl to Dead Man's Lake, several miles off the trail. Rick looked, as usual, like a peddler from the lower East Side, socks and pots dangling from his pack and belt, his Levis caked with sweat and dirt. First-timer Essie's clothes, new 3 days before, would have been rejected by Goodwill and the Salvation Army. Karen resembled a misplaced Bedouin, swathed in tattered gauzes of her own devising to shield her sensitive skin from the sun. Hal brought up the rear, the Pig Pen of the group and living proof that there's a difference between dirt (what humans create) and earth (what nature creates).

We weren't alone. Coming from the other side of the bowl was another party of 4. When we eventually met, we were astounded. They were a nice nuclear family: mom, dad and twin boys, aged 11. They were clean and tidy. In fact, they were fastidious! Mom's hair looked as if it had just been set; Dad was ready for church; the boys were exemplary behind the ears and, one supposes, everywhere else. Their clothes fit well and were spotless. We can still see Mom's lipstick, make-up and manicure. Yet these were no fancy dude-ranchers. They were experienced backpackers, had been over this arduous terrain before, carried plain efficient packs and wore modest clothes that never saw the inside of a posh sporting goods shop.

The point is, you can be as clean or "casual" as you want. One is not better than the other. However, be sensitive to the preferences of others in your party; don't make a big thing of cleanliness if the others don't agree. Also, if you intend to wash clothes, take precautions to keep the wilderness clean, too. Don't wash clothes in a lake or stream. Even without soap, they often contain detergents from previous washes. They also spew dirt into the water. Wash in pots and discard the laundry water at least 300 feet from the water source. Otherwise seepage will carry suds and dirt back to the stream or lakebed.

odds 'n ends: Individual precautions are vital. Karen is allergic to the sun. A long-sleeved cotton shirt, lightweight pants, a visor and lots of super sun-screen are necessities to keep her on the trail. Hal's thinning hair recently reached the point of no return; after a blazing sunburn on his balding head, he now wears a cap instead of a visor.

We always leave a clean shirt and underwear, fresh socks and pants in the car while we hike. They do wonders for morale when we're driving through 95 degrees toward home. And we need hardly mention what they'll do for the staff of the roadside beanery where you stop for your first indoor meal in a week.

Sleeping bags

A sleeping bag is nothing more than a heat-retaining sack to keep you warm while you're horizontal and snoozing. It needs to be efficient: the temperature of the body drops when it is at rest, and the higher the elevation, the colder both the air and the ground will be. But a sleeping bag doesn't need to be so efficient that it would keep a climber cosy on Everest; it doesn't need to be so expensive that it would make a night at the Ritz a bargain by comparison. It should be light (5 pounds or less), warm and affordable.

Sleeping bags are generally filled with down (goose or duck) or fiber. Down is warmer, lighter and more expensive. But when it's wet, it loses its insulating abilities. Fibers have various names, and are basically cheaper and heavier than down bags of the same warmth. Fibers are also much warmer when wet, because they maintain their loft. The mail-order catalogues and books mentioned in the "Appendix" contain more detailed explanations of sleeping bag construction and bag ratings according to the lowest temperatures at which they'll keep you warm.

The sleeping bag is only one part of the sandwich of warmth you need to create. If other parts of the sandwich are missing, you'll be in exactly the kind of trouble you encounter trying to eat peanut butter and jelly without any bread. Think layers. On the bottom is a ground-cloth, poncho, or reinforced tent floor. Then comes an ensolite or thin foam pad, available in a wide range of materials, lengths and thicknesses. Then the sleeping bag. Inside that is a clothed body if the bag is not very warm: the warmer the bag, the fewer the clothes. The older Hal's bargain basement special got, the more clothes he wore until one year he was forced to make a choice: get a raccoon coat or a new bag. Next comes the roof of the tent, with a rain-fly as another layer just above. Properly arranged, this sandwich is guaranteed to keep you warm and dry.

Unless you have the habits of a nocturnal arctic animal, a cold, sleepless night isn't much fun. And a wet sleeping bag almost assures a grouchy morning. If it does get wet, however, you have several options, depending on how soaked the bag is and what it's made of. If you're sleeping in the open and wake up in a dew-drenched bag, it'll often dry out an hour or 2 after the sun rises. If a thunderstorm catches you on the trail and your bag gets partially wet before you batten down the hatches, you can usually get through the night comfortably—the wet spots will be on the surface and won't penetrate the fill. If a sleeping bag really gets soaked, you've got troubles. A hot sun will dry out any bag eventually, though down takes considerably longer than fiber. But bad weather may cut off that option and the only alternative may be to share the other bags in shifts or pack up and head out. So take every precaution to keep the middle layer of your sandwich of warmth dry.

Tips

• Some sleeping bags can be zipped together to make one double bag. When buying or borrowing bags, make sure that you come away with both a left-hand and a right-hand zipper. Otherwise, even if you're with your mate, you'll be sleeping alone.

• Carry a couple repair patches. Nothing is quite so discouraging as free-flying goose or duck down. Band-Aids or adhesive tape will do the trick in a pinch.

• Be sure the stuff sack you use actually accommodates the bag. In fact, if the sack is a bit bigger, you can fit a down jacket, wool hat and flashlight — all your night-time gear — with the sleeping bag in one convenient place.

• Follow cleaning directions carefully or you may end up with a ruined sleeping bag. Hang bags on hangers or keep them on shelves when not in use. Kept in stuff sacks, they lose their loft.

• Expect to spend from $75-$160 for a good sleeping bag. Warmer, lighter bags with better zippers, materials and construction cost more; it pays to shop around.

• Finally, be patient when trying to unsnag the edge of the sleeping bag if it's caught under the zipper. It will get caught often, especially when you need to zip up or down in a hurry. To unsnag, pry apart gently in a horizontal motion. The thumbs do most of the work as they move away from each other. Don't try to unzip the snag. You'll only snag it farther, or rip the material.

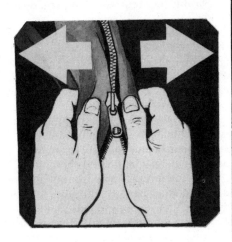

Tents

On the afternoon of the fifth day at North Lake, it began to rain. Our old, 2-person, A-frame tent was set under a tree on a slight incline. By 9:OO p.m. the tent floor, never waterproof, was soaking up ground-water like a sponge. The precautionary ditch we had tried to dig around the tent was a joke. Rain was dripping through the makeshift rain-fly we'd rigged from 2 ponchos, then it started dripping through the roof of the tent. Add 2 wet and affectionate dogs atop our sleeping bags and by morning, our tent would have made even Buffalo attractive to W.C. Fields.

The rain continued for the rest of the second day and all that night. Though wet, we kept warm and active, and by nightfall were steeled against another 8 hours of marinelife inside the tent. We finally dozed off around dawn. Later, we peeked out. It had stopped raining. Now it was snowing! We made a quick decision. Forty-eight hours in a wet tent, half frozen as well, was enough. We headed out.

Tents, like sleeping bags, come in many varieties. But there are 3 basic variables: utility, weight and cost. A tent does 2 things: It keeps out the weather and keeps out the bugs. If it accomplishes both those tasks but weighs in the neighborhood of Barnum and Bailey's Big Top it is next to useless. And if it's the right weight (no more than 7 pounds, about 3 1/2 per person), but costs as much as the bridal suite at Clar-idge's, it'll never leave the display window. You can spend as little as $95 or as much as $2OO for a 2-person tent (see "Appendix" for books and catalogues which rate and compare tents).

Shelter of some sort is desirable, but it's possible to backpack without a tent. Tie a rope between two trees and drape a tarp or poncho over it. Anchor the 4 ends to the ground, and you'll keep modestly dry. If you use a tarp, carry some light nylon cord to secure the ends. Some tarps have grommets or reinforced holes; otherwise use Vis-clamps (purchased separately) which act as portable grommets. Also useful are four metal tent stakes which can anchor a tarp to the ground. Moving beyond tarps and ponchos, there's an array of one-person tents, such as tube tents and bivouac sacks, which look more like envelopes for sleeping bags.

If you decide on a traditional A-frame tent, make sure you've got enough tent pegs to secure both the tent and its rain fly. Plastic tent pegs are useless in the high granite country; we prefer to carry metal ones. Often a tent peg is useless no matter what it's made of. Don't fret: wrap the tent line around a heavy rock or tree trunk instead.

Of the many new tent designs, the dome or geodesic tent is one of the best. It can be erected in half the time of an A-frame, without stakes or poles. The dome is suspended on 2 or more "spines," made up of collapsible fiberglass poles, and unless there's high wind, the tent doesn't have to be staked. That means you can pick up the whole tent, with sleeping bags inside, and move it into the shade for an afternoon nap, then return it to its original site for the night. Also, you can almost stand up in it, a decided advance from the old horizontal squirm required in the A-frame.

The rain-fly is an essential "extra." It fits over the roof, extends

beyond it, and is meant to carry rain water off and away from the tent sides. The rain-fly makes the tent hot—it's waterproof and doesn't "breathe." (The tent roof is not waterproof; it *does* breathe and thus allows the moisture in your sweat and breath to evaporate.) Many backpackers leave the rain-fly off until they sense rain. This is acceptable; leaving it home is not. Recent fabric innovations have created rainproof tents which allow moist air (water vapor) to escape.

Tents are susceptible to fish hooks, knife blades, sharp edges, red-hot pans, burning cigarettes and other rough treatment. The more holes in your tent, the more moisture and bugs, so it's useful to keep some patches on hand to repair damage immediately. At home, the tent should be thoroughly dried, then brushed or shaken clean and stored on a shelf or a hanger rather than in its stuff sack. One final word of advice: make sure everybody who's using the tent knows how to set it up. Let everyone take a turn at it on sunny days, so they're ready during that sudden hailstorm. Manufacturer's directions usually get lost, so learn the tricks yourself and pass them on by the old show-and-tell method.

The Versatile Garbage Bag

One more item that'll keep you dry is the garbage bag—the big garden-sized, plastic sack that you stuff fallen leaves into once or twice a year. No longer does a backpack have to be crammed into your tent during the rain; the garbage bag is a perfect protective fit. Take along as many bags as there are packs on your trip. In a pinch, if you run short of ponchos, punch some holes in one to wear for upper body protection. We buy ours as thick as they come (they're measured in "mils"). Special backpack covers are also available for very wet climates.

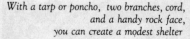
With a tarp or poncho, two branches, cord, and a handy rock face, you can create a modest shelter

Boots And Packs

Boots

When our North London friend, Brian, arrived for a quick trip to the Yosemite backcountry on his way to Alaska, he had no boots. He'd just come from hiking all over Europe — *sans* boots. And he was too broke to even think about getting some. We tried to convert him: he could use good boots in Alaska. He agreed to think it over, even went out and tried on a pair. And a day before we left, he came back all smiles from a shopping spree. He'd made the plunge. Out of a huge box he pulled a beautiful, pristine white pair of high-top basketball sneakers. He was ready for the Himalayas.

Brian made a Class 2 ascent of an 1100 foot peak ("Class 2" is mountaineering for moderately difficult), took 2 rough cross country trips to Crystal Lake, went on a 4-hour solo adventure down a tributary of the local river, carried a heavy pack, and got nary a blister or sore foot from his high-tops. Hal's daughter, Annika, did a 5-day trip in a pair of boots meant for city snow wear. And her friend Kelly, loath to shell out too much money before she knew if she'd really like backpacking, hiked comfortably in tennis shoes.

It's possible to backpack seriously in rough terrain in almost any kind of comfortable footwear that has some sort of rubberized sole and a modicum of support. Good mountaineering boots are used — and useful — because they're sturdier than other kinds of shoes; last better under the punishing treatment they receive in mountain terrain; give support to ankles and feet that are subjected to heavy loads and unexpected twists and turns; and provide traction on steep rock faces and other quirks of nature not found on Main Street. Brian, for all his agility, came out of the mountains minus those new sneakers — they'd been ripped to shreds. Kelly will never play tennis again in her tennies, and Annika is hard put to keep the snow out of those poor over-abused boots.

The message is: don't be intimidated if you don't have and can't afford a pair of super-ace Mountain Goat expedition boots. Don't stay at home just because you feel unshod. However, if you can afford decent mountaineering boots, you won't be throwing away mutilated sneakers every year after 5 days in the wilderness. You'll be more confident in off-trail situations where traction is vital. You'll probably be more secure carrying a heavy pack. Cared for properly, good boots will last a long time—often 5 to 10 years, depending on how you and the terrain are on them.

Aside from the appropriateness of the boot (you don't want technical mountaineering boots, unless of course you're a technical mountaineer) and cost, the all-important consideration is size. Get it right. You and your backpacking mates will regret it if you don't. To get the right boot and fit, depend on the experts. The books and catalogues in the "Appendix" discuss Vibram soles, steel shanks, Norwegian welts and outside stitchdowns, one-piece uppers, rough-out leather, as well as the new generation of light-weight synthetic hiking boots, and just about anything else you've always wanted to know about the inner mysteries of outdoor footwear. But keep in mind that it's best to try on boots with a knowledgeable salesperson to help determine choice and fit, and to wear the same socks (or 2 socks) you'll be wearing in the mountains. Boots are one of the few items that are hard to rent. So the money you spend—at least $65 and more likely nearly $100—is a long-term investment. Plunge wisely, watch for sales, and see if the salesperson will bargain.

Install fresh, strong laces before the trip. If a lace breaks on the trail, knot it and carry on. If the whole thing shrivels and dies, rig up a lace out of a length of that nylon cord you're carrying.

When you get home from each trip, clean your boots and treat them with boot oil. Store in a cool, dry place with crumpled up newspapers inside to absorb moisture. Before your next trip, coat them with Sno-Seal, a wax-like oil which makes them more water resistant for stream crossings or hiking in mud and rain.

The subject of boots inevitably leads to the subject of blisters. No matter how perfect the fit or how expert the wearer, blisters can strike almost any time. New boots, an extra-long day of hiking, a continuous downhill stretch, wet or dirty socks, an inadvertent abrasion on the heel or toe—the causes of blisters are endless. To be prepared, carry enough moleskin (the trade name of a lightly padded adhesive plaster) to service everyone on the trip. One packet per person is generous. To cut moleskin to the desired shapes, scissors far surpass a knife. Some people prefer their moleskin doughnut-shaped, with the blister in the center. Others use Band-Aids, or gauze and tape.

Packs

According to Funk and Wagnalls, "backpacking" means packing things on the back. To do this efficiently and with reasonable comfort, you need a frame pack. A frame pack consists of a lightweight frame, usually made of aluminum or an aluminum alloy, from which is suspended a large nylon bag, often divided into compartments and pouches. The frame goes on you, via padded shoulder straps and waist bands. The load, packed in the bag, goes on the frame and is separated from you by a back band. No part of the load touches any part of you. The principle is to distribute weight evenly between shoulders and hips, and a good pack will permit you, by strap adjustments, to shift weight from your shoulders to your hips in varying degrees.

Camping stores stock a bewildering variety of backpacks: top-loading, back-loading, single-compartment, divided compartment, adjustable waist-suspension systems, and on and on. They also have a large variety of non-frame or ''soft'' packs, from small daypacks and book bags to large non-frame ones used for bicycling and cross-country skiing (activities requiring a hunched back or swinging shoulders) as well as for traveling. Again, weight, utility, comfort and cost are your guiding factors. Research and shop carefully. Most adult packs weigh from 4½-5½ pounds. With anything lighter, either the frame will be weak (poor welds, cheap alloys), or the pack will be made of material too fragile to sustain a heavy load. Anything much heavier, you won't want to carry.

Be sure to try on several packs. Frame sizes differ and it's important to get the frame made for your height and build—most packs come in small, medium, large and extra large. Make sure the frame has room below or above the pack for strapping on a sleeping bag, tent, ensolite pad, and other gear. Think also about how much you plan to carry. It won't make sense to buy a huge 5,000-cubic-inch pack if you can only handle the weight that would fit into a 2,500-cubic-inch pack. Ask the salesperson to load up the pack so you can test it for weight. See how it feels on your shoulders. Check out the number of compartments and side pouches. A single-compartment, top-loading bag may be the one you like, but if it doesn't have a back-loading zipper panel as well, every time you want something stashed down at the bottom, you'll be pulling everything out. Look at the suspension system, how the bag hangs on the frame. Can the bag be moved for body adjustments? Can the hip or waist bands be altered? Can a missing part (pin, bolt or back band) be fixed or replaced? Check for soft padding on shoulder straps and hip belts. And expect to pay, unless you rent, between $75 and $125 for a quality pack. Among the brand names that you can trust are Kelty, Camp Trails, R.E.I. and Jansport.

Wear and tear on packs shows first in the fastenings. Zippers and their fittings fray; half-rings and tie-cord loops disappear; key wires work loose from clevis pins; nylon bags rip. With some care, however, a good backpack should last for years. Necessary repairs can be made cheaply. A little WD-4O lubricant spray, available in auto parts stores, should be applied to all zippers before leaving home; frayed nylon strands that get caught in zippers can be trimmed with scissors or sealed with a match flame; rings and wires can be fashioned out of everything from bailing wire to paper clips; bags can be patched and sewn. Weakened or broken frames can be rewelded ("heliarced" with aluminum alloys); on the trail they can be patched together with cord, fishing line and ingenuity.

Packs For The Pooch

Let your dog do its part of the work when backpacking. If weight is evenly distributed over its sides, most dogs can and will pack a modest amount, at least as much as they'll eat. Thus they can carry their own food into the wilderness and, as it diminishes, can take out your supplies (garbage, shoes, whatever can be symmetrically paired). Dog packs cost around $4O. They consist of 2 oblong carrying sacks made of treated nylon with a tough canvas or leather underside fixed to a strong nylon "saddle" that fits on the dog's back. The sacks are suspended over the dogs's flanks in a manner that will not chafe its legs or sides while on the trail. Straps fit around the chest and under the belly.

We use home-made versions of the commercial model for our small

dogs. Two rubberized canvas sacks or small reinforced stuff sacks from an army surplus store, 2 lengths of strap and 4 large safety pins are all that's needed, plus the patience to sew the parts together with heavy carpet thread. The safety pins are used to close the sack openings.

Rover doesn't need special training to carry a pack, though a dry run helps get the pooch used to that strange unseen burden. Remember to keep the dog on a leash whenever the pack is on, even when you stop to rest. Otherwise, on the first scent of deer or chipmunk, dog and pack will disappear. Dog will most likely return, but pack almost assuredly will not. If it does, it may be minus its contents: rocks and brush can rip it to shreds. Off the trail, remove the dog packs and carry them yourself. And unless your pooch's pack is watertight, expect the bottom of the pack and its contents to get wet when crossing shallow streams and rivulets.

Stoves And Fuel

Among the several basic types of backpacking stoves, white gas, kerosene, and bottled gas (propane or butane) are the most popular. Alcohol stoves are cheap, but so inefficient they're not worth it; and Sterno, which is light, is impossible to control. Since there's a wide and technical range to choose from, we suggest you study the literature and get face-to-face advice from someone who has actually used these stoves. Then check them out in person. If possible, rent and use one before buying. Some questions to consider:

- What kind of fuel?
- How complicated to use?
- Can you trim it to a low flame for simmering?
- How much fuel does it consume?
- How much does it weigh?
- What is likely to go wrong?
- Can you fix/clean it with the tool(s) you have along?

White gas stoves are popular because the fuel ignites fast and burns hot. They're easy to use. Many require no pumping to vaporize the fuel, which can be carried in easy-to-pack aluminum or plastic containers. Its disadvantages? White gas is volatile, which is what makes it ignite so easily. It needs to be handled with care so it doesn't burn unexpectedly; and fuel containers need to be vented periodically so that pressure doesn't build up. Also, white gas may be difficult to find, though hardware and camping stores stock it or a substitute called camping or Coleman fuel. Chevron gas stations sell it as "Blazo."

Kerosene ignites more slowly but burns hotter. It's thus potentially safer and more efficient. It is also almost universally available and cheap. Its drawbacks are—it stinks, it stains and it's hard to start when it is cold. Furthermore, it requires another fuel, such as denatured alcohol, as a primer, and needs pumping to obtain vaporizing pressure in the fuel tank. In short, kerosene stoves are rarely worth the hassle.

Many white gas and all kerosene stoves need priming to start. This means the stove must be pre-heated with extra fuel so the gas in the tank will vaporize, expand and force its way into the burner in a steady flow. To prime a stove, extract some fuel from the fuel container—*not the stove's tank*—with an eyedropper or plastic tube, place it in the bowl of the stove beneath the vaporizer, light it, and, as it burns, open the control valve. This starts up the burner—or it's supposed to. If it doesn't, begin the whole operation over again. Don't overfill the bowl. And remember, cold weather inhibits vaporizing, so it may be harder to start your stove in the mountains than in your backyard.

Bottled gas stoves are so easy to use that you'd think they'd have long since replaced all the others. The fuel—propane or butane—is purchased in a pressurized cartridge. When it's attached to the stove, all you do is turn on the valve, light up and cook. No pumping, no priming, no muss, no fuss. The flame is more finely adjustable than on the gasoline stoves. However, the fuel can be hard to find and is more expensive. It doesn't burn as hot, which means you need more of it to get the same amount of work done, and the stove's efficiency decreases in direct proportion to the amount of fuel left in the cartridge. Four days into the mountains you'll have to cook longer and longer to get a meal done. Propane and butane also have an embarrassing tendency to revert into liquids when it's cold, or freeze solid if the temperature really hits bottom. Butane liquifies at 10 degrees F, propane at -45 degrees F. If the weather threatens to turn you blue, it will turn your gas blue too. Take a fuel cartridge to bed; sleeping bag warmth will help keep it in firing condition. And 2 final things: Once a fuel cartridge is attached to the stove, it can't be removed until it's empty; a puncture hole in the cartridge allows the gas to escape into the stove. It will escape all over the environment if you remove it. This may be cumbersome for packing purposes if you're moving on with a half-empty cartridge. And of course you have to pack out the used cylinders.

Your actual "mileage" may vary, but with a little higher mathematics you can get a ballpark estimate of how much fuel you'll need. First, count the meals. Say you're going for 7 days. On the first and last days

Optimus 111B (white gas); Bleuet S200S (butane); Optimus 00 (kerosene).

you'll need only one hot meal, on the other 5, you need 2. Altogether, 12 hot meals. Assume you use 1/2-hour of fuel for each meal. That's extravagant—some of your meals will be those "add hot water and serve" affairs. But better to have more fuel than less, especially for that last unforseen banquet of 6 big trout and trimmings. So in all, 6 hours of cooking. If you're using a small white gas stove, say an Optimus 323 Purist 1, the tank will hold .35 pint which gives about 45 minutes of cooking at full flame. Conclusion: take along 3 pints of fuel, packed in a one-liter and a half-liter bottle—heavy but manageable. Say, on the other hand, that you're using a butane-burning Bleuet S200. Six hours will use most, or all of, 2 cartridges.

Ever notice the people in those rosy-hued camping stove ads are always smiling? That's because their stoves work! It'll be cold comfort in the mountains if you can't get your Promethean Mountain Model going when you need that hot cup of brew to get *you* going. Know how your stove works. Practice starting it at home. If you get burned, better it should be in the backyard than on a lonely precipice. And learn to save fuel. The most efficient and brilliant menu in the world won't warm the cockles of anybody's heart if you can't heat the pot. Don't fire up till you see the whites of their eggs!

Regardless of make and model, here are some other things to keep in mind. First, fuel contaminates food. Pack it separately from your edibles. Wrap the fuel container in a plastic bag or two. Then, even if it seeps a little or cracks when, for example, your pack drops on the ground, the food stays safe. Second, *fuel is volatile;* keep it away from heat sources other than your stove. Release the vapor pressure in fuel containers and the stove's tank occasionally as you climb. Never refuel a stove while it's hot. Third, stoves need ventilation; give them air. Be careful cooking in a tent. Many tents are flammable; only recently have laws required tents to be made of flame resistant materials. Make sure yours has been treated before cooking inside it. Even then, open tent flaps and keep the stove near an exit. A large pot on a small stove may also prevent proper ventilation and cause overheating. Fourth, stoves work best when set on a flat surface and protected from the wind. Cook on a flat rock or smooth ground in the lee of a tree or boulder, or make a wind baffle out of a circle of rocks or aluminum foil fashioned into a cylinder that fits around the stove with enough ventilation space.

Oh, and one more thing. Don't forget your matches.

Fixing Things And Mending Bodies

Repairs

If all that expensive gear breaks down on the trail, the one-year guarantees won't be worth the proverbial paper. You either live with the problem or fix it. We've never seen a backpacking trip where everything worked right; something invariably breaks, tears, rips or malfunctions. A good repair kit is essential.

- Vise Grips
- Needle and thread
- Safety pins
- Spare clevis pins and key wires (for the backpack)
- Spare flashlight batteries and bulbs
- 5O' of nylon cord
- Roll of 1/2 inch adhesive tape
- Swiss army knife (''Tinker'' model)

Patience and ingenuity are also required to make adequate repairs; these are both a matter of attitude. Make the job challenging and fun. Sit in a shady place, unpack the repair kit and ponder the problem. Use your imagination. Take frequent breaks if the job is tedious. Once Hal's boot sole started to come apart. He got out the large needle, pushed it through the rubber and leather with a rock, then pulled it the rest of the way with the vise grips. On another trip a backpack frame broke. We trimmed a branch to fit inside the hollow tubes, butted the broken pieces against each other with the branch as a reinforcing rod, then taped and retied the frame back together. Another time, a low-hanging branch snapped Rick's fishing rod in half. He found that one section of the hollow fiberglass tubing slid right into the other. So he looped the thick carpet thread around the break to keep the pieces together. Using only the Swiss army knife and vise grips, we've even disassembled and reassembled our backpacking stove. Ripped packs, broken sunglasses, sticky fishing reels: all have been repaired. Finally, don't worry if you make something worse while trying to fix it. Even the most resourceful jack or jill of all trades occasionally packs out a broken article. If, however, you work slowly and carefully and have some basic tools and supplies, you can usually do an adequate job.

First Aid Kit

Our first aid kit has never really been tested. We've never had a major medical or first aid problem on a trip. All we can tell you is what we take and what we've used. There are good books on backpacking first aid which you may want to look at. We especially recommend Dick Mitchell's *Mountaineering First Aid*. Beyond that we suggest you get in touch with local authorities regarding any special medical preparations for your trip (for example, contaminated water in a particular area may require purification tablets or boiling).

We routinely use lots of aspirin on backpacking trips. It relieves headaches caused by sun, lack of salt, altitude or fatigue. It also helps aching muscles. Band-Aids and moleskin, both of which may be found liberally attached to our feet, are the other two items always in high demand from the first aid kit.

The rest of our supplies are rarely touched, but they're there, just in case. We bring several square gauze bandages, strong tweezers for splinters, adhesive tape and needle (from the repair kit), codeine for serious pain, decongestant, lomotil for diarrhea, antacid for upset stomachs and antibiotic pills in case of a strep throat. A salve, first aid cream or disinfectant is also useful. Some people bring Ace Bandages for strained or swollen ankles or knees. When backpacking alone, add a mirror in case something gets in your eye.

Individuals should carry whatever medicines they need. Karen wouldn't be caught in Carlsbad Caverns without a good sunscreen, while Hal would sooner go into the mountains without boots than leave his back pills behind. Mary brings sulfa drugs in case of a urinary infection and Rick is addicted to Vitamin C. Don't skimp on what's necessary for you.

There are two other necessary items: Chap-stick and hand lotion. Hot weather, cold winds, and constant exposure to the elements really dry out face, hands and lips. A nightly application of lotion goes a long way toward preventing that loss of moisture, as does a daily dose of

Chap-stick. After one trip when it becomes painful to move your hands or lips, you'll never forget either of these items again.

The great snake bite question inevitably arises. We can give you a few hints. In 15 years of backpacking in California, the Rockies and the Southwest, we've never seen a poisonous snake, nor heard one rattle. Snakes are as terrified of you as you are of them. Statistically, the number of fatalities from snake bites in the U.S. is so small as to be almost negligible: about 30 people, mostly small children, die each year from snake venom.

The snake bite kit itself (razor blade, tourniquet and disinfectant) is a two-edged sword. "Authorities generally advise carrying a snake-bite kit, but in unpracticed hand of semi-hysterical first-aiders, the kit can be more dangerous than the bite; the rule is to seek instruction before entering an area where it may be needed." (Harvey Manning, *Backpacking, One Step at a Time,* p. 52.) We used to carry a bite kit, but it seems to have disappeared in recent years and we haven't replaced it. There are very few snakes over 7,000 feet (where we backpack), but rattlesnakes might be a danger in other areas. Check before you go. If in snake country, be sure to wear long pants and heavy boots.

What about serious injuries: a broken leg, a case of pneumonia, a wound needing sutures? In the first place, these are most dangerous when alone. If you and your pack fall into an icy river late one rainy, windy afternoon, there is real danger of hypothermia. Alone, you're in the same fix as a solo climber who falls and breaks a leg. Anytime you go off by yourself, whether exploring or climbing, be sure someone knows exactly what your plans are and where you'll be. And come back on time, even if that means not making it to your destination.

The second rule is not to move seriously injured victims. Set up a campsite that is as warm and dry as possible. Then go for help. Most ranger stations have helicopters available for life-threatening emergencies. Rangers are rarely more than 2 or 3 slow hiking days away (1 long day without a pack). If the injured person can be left in comfortable surroundings, you can usually have a doctor there within 24 hours. Don't try to carry anyone out over rough terrain.

What To Take

Out there somewhere may be a monster of total recall who can keep in mind everything necessary for a mountain trip. But that's not us. We keep lists. Lots of lists. Lists for food, equipment, replacement items within the equipment list (such as the first aid kit and repair kit); we even make a list of the lists we need to make. That sounds like a lot of trouble, but since our requirements don't vary much from trip to trip or year to year, once one is made it can be used almost forever. Just keep a master list in reasonably good shape in your map drawer. We have several lists in the book: fishing gear (pp. 118-120), food and cooking gear (pp.48, 50, 52-54), repair kit (above, p. 34), and accessories (see below and p. 38). The lists will grow or shrink occasionally, according to group size and needs. And it's a good idea to keep a spare copy handy to jot down items you think of before, during and after your trips.

Group Accessories

So many things can be shared that they become group accessories rather than private necessities. Some things everyone should have, while other things individual members may want. Here's a list of items we take as shared goods:

• Maps, star map, tree finding guide and compass.
• Two boxes kitchen matches with sulphur heads (strike anywhere).
• First aid kit and repair kit.
• Tooth paste, dental floss.
• Liquid (biodegradable) dish soap and pot scrubber.
• Mosquito repellent (two bottles).
• Paper and pencil.
• Camera and film.
• Extra pack straps.
• Garbage bags (one for each member of the party).
• Extra Ziploc bags (10-12).
• Extra tent pegs.
• Extra tarps (one for every two people).
• Backpacking saw.
• Book for reading aloud.
• Two-person inflatable backpacking raft plus paddles (when other weight considerations permit).

Someone recently asked us how much toilet paper we take on a backpacking trip. It was a poignant question. The answer is, ''enough to satisfy everybody's expected needs.'' This includes cleaning pots, polishing glasses, sometimes lighting a fire, as well as the manufacturer's recommended use. We've found that 2 rolls are adequate for a 10 day trip for 2. But we've known people to sneak in an extra roll—''just in case.''

Individual Needs

Everyone should have the following:

- Pocket knife.
- Sun glasses (in hard case).
- Matches (in plastic bag or already waterproofed).
- Flashlight (such as Mallory AA compact flashlight or another weighing about 3 oz. with batteries, and which can be held in the mouth when both hands are needed).
- Caution: Remove batteries before storing for winter. This will avoid a corroded, ruined flashlight 6 months later.

Other things are optional in the eyes of some, but essential in the eyes of others:

- Water bottle.
- Ring clip to carry the car keys.
- Fishing license.
- Camera and film.
- Paperback book.
- Toothbrush, toothpaste, comb, barettes, ponytail bands.
- Towel and bar of (biodegradable) soap.
- Sanitary napkins, tampons, sponges, etc.
- Birth control devices.
- Glasses case and extra glasses.
- Contact lens solution.
- Personal medications or prescriptions.
- Nail clippers.
- Playing cards, chess set, etc.
- Security blanket, stuffed animal, etc. (Hal's daughter Stanya brought her battered old baby blanket above 10,000 feet on several occasions. It was always necessary.)

But some things, however desirable, should not be brought into the wilderness: deodorants, perfumes and other scented cosmetics, which all attract insects and some of which attract bears; cassette recorders and other machines which can disturb other packers' searches for solitude; and guns which can only be used to hurt people or other living things.

The Library

One of our great pleasures on backpacking trips is reading aloud.

We find so much time for it—during a rest break on the trail, while preparing one of our elaborate meals, while one of us is fishing, or just while hanging out—that over the years we've digested some of the world's longest books. As we read, we burn, that way we don't have to carry the book's weight out.

The best books for this kind of reading are long, episodic stories where it doesn't matter if you miss a paragraph or even a chapter. Among our favorites have been Mark Twain's *Huckleberry Finn* and *A Connecticut Yankee at King Arthur's Court*, John Barth's *The Sotweed Factor, Bleak House* by Charles Dickens (over 900 pages!), Henry Fielding's *Tom Jones* (a lot funnier and longer than the movie), the short stories of P.G. Wodehouse and Ring Lardner, the mystery novels of Dashiell Hammett and a good collection of ghost stories. In short, bring anything you enjoy—magazines, comic books, joke books, box tops, and any other printed material you won't mind burning or packing out—crosswords, games, mantras, amulets, recipes— whatever tickles your fancy.

Weight

Lists weigh next to nothing, but equipment doesn't. If all that nicely assembled gear is too heavy to move out of the living room, you might as well stay home. Just how much you can carry depends on your own weight, height, physical condition, state of mind, and on the facilities you have for carrying a load: a strong and big pack, a strong and little pack, or a weak, fragile pack. It also depends on how long the trip is and how many people will be sharing the load. Putting all these ingredients in the hopper and shaking, we've determined the "average load" for an "average adult" for a 4-person trip for 6 days, door to door: 34 pounds. Of this, food will weigh about 7 1/4 pounds per person (1 1/2 lbs./person/day, excluding the first and last travel days). Non-food weight will be about 26 3/4 pounds, including water and the weight of the empty pack itself. As trips get longer, food takes up a greater percentage of total weight, and other things, like the inflatable raft, 35 mm. camera, or the frying pan, may have to go.

If you take something extravagant, like the inflatable raft and paddles, each person needs to add a little more weight to the pack load. That doesn't mean everyone will carry equal weight. Somebody will haul nearly 45 pounds and someone else closer to 25 pounds. That's OK. If there are only 2 of you, you'll each carry a lot more (excluding the raft), for a minimum total of just over 39 pounds.

How much can one person carry? A good guide is to begin with 20 percent of your body weight. If you're in good shape, you can raise that to 25 percent. A group of 160-pound joggers can easily carry 40 pounds each. But if 3 of your 4-person group weigh less than 120 pounds, you might have to start cutting corners to reduce their packs to 25 pounds or so.

Maps And Permits

Maps

There are 2 types of maps you need to plan your trip: a topographical map ("topo map") which provides an accurate picture of the terrain, showing elevation and distances; and the general maps put out by whoever supervises the area: National or State Park or Forest Services. Forest and Park Service maps are updated every 10 years or so, showing changes in access roads, jeep trails, campgrounds, parking areas and new hiking trails. Since mountains and valleys aren't likely to change much, topo maps, which can be 50 years old, don't need revision. With both, you're ready to start charting routes.

Topo maps are obtained from a U.S. Geological Survey office in the area. For example, the San Francisco office sells maps of California mountains; the Denver office sells maps of the Rocky Mountains; eastern offices sell maps of East Coast mountain ranges. The maps are also available by mail (see "Appendix" for addresses). But you'll first need to send for a free "key" or index map, which shows the whole state divided into small squares. Each of these squares is numbered and titled, representing one topo map. After you pinpoint an area, you can send for the relevant maps by number and title.

Maps of the National and State parks and forests have to be obtained from the appropriate agency office (see "Appendix"). Sometimes you can do this with a phone call, and the maps will be sent to you free. Other times, you have to send a check or money order. You'll find that the more camping and backpacking you do, the less you need to send for maps—not because you use them less, but because you'll keep returning to the same parks and forests. If you take good care of maps, they last forever.

Permits

It's best to apply for your permit after you've looked at the maps and decided exactly where you want to go. Permits are obtained from the local ranger station, allowing local supervisors to keep daily track of how many people enter each part of their area. The number of back-country travelers is growing rapidly. It's not unusual for 200 people per day to pass some scenic spots on the John Muir Trail in Sequoia National Park, for example. Park officials keep tabs in order to avoid over-crowding and destruction. They also need to know where you are in case of an emergency, such as a fire.

There's another reason to get permits in advance. Along with the permit, you'll get any information the rangers feel is important to pass on. This includes warnings about bears in the area, cautions involving drinking water and possible disease transmission, notices of areas closed to camping, and rules regarding firewood, fires and fishing. These are all vital to learn about before you arrive with your bulging backpack, only to discover, say, that you've overlooked the water purification tablets.

It's possible to get permits at the last minute, but rules differ. In some areas, you can arrive at a ranger station, get a permit immediately, drive to the trailhead and begin hiking. Other times you can telephone ahead and the permit will be waiting for you in the pick-up box outside the ranger station door for late-night arrivals. Still other times you'll find that the trail is full for the day; permits will be issued for the following day only. It pays to have alternate routes and destinations in mind for just such eventualities. One year, we reached a National Forest area in the evening, planning to get our permit the following morning. A sign in front of the ranger station said that half the permits were issued in advance by mail (only until the end of April). The rest were issued that day, with the last few to be distributed at 6 a.m. the next morning. We approached the ranger station at 5:45, to find ourselves behind nearly 40 other earlier risers. Our first choice was booked solid, and we had to settle for a second-choice route.

It's best to plan your trip well in advance. Order maps during rainy winter afternoons; send for July and August permits in March. Especially if you're planning a week-long trip, the more time you give yourself, the smoother it will go. It's possible to backpack "spontaneously" but trips invariably work out better if they are thought out and arranged months in advance.

CHAPTER III: Food

Food Weights And Planning

Our friend Lowell used to be an ace backcountry hiker. Then he became a letter carrier on the hills of San Francisco. He soon grew weary of his busman's holidays and retired from backpacking in favor of his work. But on the trail he was good, and often did things his own way. Where others wore the latest hiking boots, he'd lead the way down rock falls in a pair of battered basketball hightops. When others pressed grimly toward the destination in afternoon's hottest sunshine, he'd find the deepest shade available, unroll his ensolite pad and sleep out the heat, often arriving at the campsite by flashlight. And where the rest of us were satisfied with dried foods and soup packets, he insisted on packing in fresh onions, potatoes, carrots, turnips and other weighty produce for his cherished stews.

Then there's Rob, who lives on rice and oatmeal cooked in a coffee can, raisins, seeds and other bird food so he can carry along his camera and telephoto lenses. The message? If you really want to bring something badly enough, you'll bring it and enjoy it, even though it seems to defy all the obvious logic of backpacking. This logic insists that food is heavy. Especially food with a high water content. If you filled your pack with onions, you'd need a forklift to get it up on your back. Food is also bulky and packs have just so much space.

Unless you pump iron for a living or are related to a burro, weight and space will dictate how much and what kind of food you can take on a mountain trip. So will distance and taste. When all the variables are considered and combined, the figures work out something like this: an average pack loaded with everything except food will weigh in the neighborhood of 27 pounds. To this will be added about 1½ pounds of food per person per day, the accepted median limit of food weight in most backpacking circles. Jewish mothers, the L.A. Raiders' front 4, and Lowell with his stews may insist on 2 pounds per day, but any more than that and you'd better sign up for weight training. Actually, we begin with the goal of a pound a day and grudgingly go up the extra ½ pound when we can't part with the Kahlua or matzoh meal. If you go exclusively with freeze-dried foods, of course, your cooking utensils will be cut to one pot, plus stove and fuel, which permits greater food weight. Anything much below a pound a day verges on nuts and berries—the school of caloric deprivation. For the sake of argument and a contented after-dinner glow, let's take 1½ and see how it adds up.

A 5 day trip will mean a 37½ pound pack; an 8-day trip, a 42-pound pack and 2 weeks, a 51-pound pack. That's a lot to schlep up a hill. Beyond that, plan to cache some food or get resupplied. If you don't believe us, put 50 pounds of rocks (or onions, we're not fussy) in a backpack and walk up 2 flights of stairs. Welcome to the reality of weight watching.

Those 1½ pounds a day include everything you'll ingest—as well as packaging containers—staples, ready-to-eat foods, spices, cooking oil. Thus, another law of backpacking logic is: the lighter the container, the more food you can carry. Check out the *net* weights on food packets when you shop. That gives you the amount of actual food in a package, as distinct from total shelf weight, which includes wrapping, cardboard, plastic and puffed-up space. With few exceptions, everything will need to be repacked in the lightest wrapping anyway, so the net weight becomes the operative figure in calculating those 1½ pounds.

Before going to the market or camping store, figure out how many meals you'll be having and where you'll be having them: on the trail (simple and quick) or in camp (complex and leisurely). You needn't know precisely what you'll be eating for every meal, just what will be available for as many hot meals as you'll need. Of course, if you like to plan menus, do so; there are lots of suggested ones in the literature. Since we're never sure if we'll want minestrone on Tuesday or lunch (at all) on Wednesday, we fudge on the menus and prepare with an eye toward improvising. That, however, does not mean spur-of-the-moment. And to illustrate the point, we show you how we planned three different trips in the summer of 1981. We even include the mistakes.

One last piece of advice: many backpackers recommend having extra quantities of emergency high-protein food: milk powder, soup, or bouillon cubes. Should you get caught in an early snowstorm for 2 unexpected days, that could be vital to pull you through.

A 6-Day Trip For 4 Plus 2 Dogs

The more you know about your appetites, abilities and the conditions at your destination, the better you plan a food inventory. You're already familiar with the first 2: you know what and how much you like to eat, and can gauge your physical ability to carry weight. Conditions, however, are likely to change: someone may get sick and not be able to eat what's available; the fishing may be lousy; the salami may be left in the fridge at home by mistake; the bears may get to dinner #3 before you do. By assessing the knowables, and expecting the variables, you're better prepared to improvise. What follows is a summary of our pre-trip considerations and how things in fact worked out.

how much weight? We were 2 adults with backpacking experience, large packs and ability to carry a lot of weight; and 2 first-time teenagers, 15 and 16, strong and healthy, with medium-sized packs. Rick and Hal carried about 47-pound packs, Annika and Kelly managed around 25 pounds apiece. The dogs carried their own food, about 7 pounds each.

dietary considerations? Everyone was fairly easy to please. On the whole, more sweets, gorp and dried fruit were added to satisfy adolescent cravings. Two days into the wilderness we learned that Kelly hated cheese and didn't much like fish. She did, however, become a convert to trout crepes and souffles by the end of the trip.

fishing prospects? Fair to good. We hadn't visited the area for 8 years. While it was great then, the number of people using the trails had grown exponentially and we could expect a lot of fishing pressure on the 4 lakes we'd visit. Additionally, they were close to the trailhead and easily accessible to day hikers. The weather was heat-wave hot and the fish might be staying deep. On the other hand, we were packing an inflatable raft which would give us an advantage. To play it safe, we didn't count on adding fish to our diet. As it turned out, we had good luck and caught enough trout for 4 hot meals.

fires permitted? Since it was early in the dry season, fires were allowed. Heavily traveled trails promised scarce firewood, but we decided not to take a stove. We found, in fact, that wood was easily accessible in all but one campsite, and even there, was available at a distance.

how many hot meals? We planned 4 hot dinners and 3 hot breakfast/lunches. Here's how it broke down:

day 1: Travel day, with breakfast at home, lunch in the car, and dinner (fried chicken and macaroni salad prepared at home and carried in a cooler) at the trailhead campground. No fire necessary.

day 2: Breakfast at campground, finishing the food we prepared at home. Lunch on the trail, with hot dinner (#1) that evening.

day 3: Start early with a quick, cold breakfast. Lunch on the trail and hot dinner (#2) that night. In fact this plan was altered. We caught 3 big fish after dinner on the second day and had them for a hot breakfast on day 3.

day 4: Hot breakfast (#1), lunch on the trail, and hot dinner (#3) that night.

day 5: Hot breakfast (#2), lunch on the trail and hot dinner (#4) at campsite. Unfortunately, it didn't work out that way at all. When we arrived at our planned destination in mid-afternoon of day 4, we found a pretty lake, a gorgeous campsite, nary a soul, and four billion voracious mosquitos. We stayed the night, but fled first thing in the morning, leaving our plans for a day of serious hanging out in shambles. No hot breakfast. Instead we retreated to another lake in time for lots of fishing and hot dinner (#4).

day 6: Our last day began with a fish fry breakfast (#3), lunch on the trail and dinner at the first steak house on the road home. This worked as planned, except that the girls set out with no food in their packs, figuring to walk with us and get to the car before eating. They forged ahead without lunch, not realizing how far 6 miles is on an empty stomach and arrived at the car famished.

The overall plan for the trip worked out reasonably well, the unplanned hot breakfast on day 3 standing in for the unplanned cold breakfast on day 5. Note that this pre-trip planning did not specify any afternoons of baking; in fact we did a lot. We made breads or cakes on the afternoons of days 2, 3, 4 and 5.

What To Bring?

It's finally time to shop. You've discussed likes and dislikes, determined how much or how little cooking you'll do, how much money you can spend, what kind of hot meals you want, what munchies are absolutely indispensable. You have a preliminary shopping list, then checked off what items you already have at home. Your first target is the supermarket — it's cheaper than specialty stores and carries all kinds of heat-and-serve foods. If there's a bulk-food store in town, you'll probably shop there for grains, flours, dried fruits, nuts and the like. If there's a camping store, you may head there for the latest in freeze-dried foods. If you do, however, bring along a shopping bag full of money; freeze-dried fare is expensive.

You won't be Ace Market's favorite customer if you ask for "one pound 11½ ounces of cookies, please, and throw in 7½ ounces of flour, will you?" Weigh out the amounts at home after you've done the shopping (see "Weighing Food," below.). If you buy too much, save it; it won't spoil.

The list on the following page shows what we assembled for our trip. The net weights, in pounds and ounces, represent what we

Large pot and small lid combine to make a wilderness double boiler

FOOD FOR A 6-DAY, 4-PERSON TRIP

Staples	Pounds	Ounces
2 doz. eggs	2	13½
2 sticks magarine		8
Cooking oil		12
Maple Syrup	1	1½
Flour	1	11
Rice	1	
Beans		7
Corn Meal		5
Sugar		8
Milk powder		4½
Onion		3½
Baking powder		2
Yeast		1½
Garlic		2
Popcorn		5½
Spices and condiments*	1	6½
Subtotal	11	11½

Ready To Eat	Pounds	Ounces
1 Italian Salami	1	4½
Cheese (assorted)	1	11
4 packets dry soup mix		14
Coffee (instant)		4½
Swiss Miss chocolate drink	1	
Cookies	1	11½
Crackers (Rykrisp, Saltines)		14
24 Tiger's Milk Bars	3	6
Chocolate (Baker's semi, German sweet)	1	
Granola		8
Brandy		9
Freeze-dried dinners for 2 days	1	5½
2 Freeze-dried desserts	1	1
Gorp (mixed nuts, dried fruit, carob chips...)	2	
Subtotal	17	8
TOTAL NET WEIGHT	29	3½

Dog food for 2 dogs, 4 days 6 lbs.

* Soy sauce, Chinese sesame oil, lemon juice, Tabasco, vinegar, dry
mustard, curry, mixed Italian herbs, cinnamon, nutmeg, pepper, salt

took, not what we bought. Also, it only represents what went to the trailhead, not what went into our packs; we made some last-minute changes. We left behind all the freeze-dried dinners and one of the freeze-dried desserts: too heavy, given our other goodies and the amount of time we planned to spend hanging out. The salami was also left behind—Hal forgot it in San Francisco when we left at 5 a.m. A third of the crackers was also left, too hot to think about all those dry biscuits. That got us down to about 27 pounds. We added another ½ pound of dried fruits and nuts, and, as a treat despite their weight (another pound), 4 oranges and 2 apples for the first day's trek. Those 28½ pounds stood us just fine, and even if we'd caught nary a fish, we'd have had more than enough to eat. We walked out on day 6 with some some cheese and crackers for lunch and arrived at the car with a single Tiger's Milk Bar as a surprise treat before hitting the road.

Second, the list does not include the fried chicken, macaroni salad, fresh fruit and juice we brought in the cooler for our travel day's snacks and meal. Don't forget to shop for those indispensables at the same time. The food in the cooler accounts for the first 3 meals of the trip (depending on how far you drive), so plan accordingly.

Third, there's the dog food to explain. If a dog goes lame or the terrain gets too rough, you'll have to carry its food, so the weight is at least marginally important. We only account for 4 days' food for the dogs. That's because we carry dry food for them for the travel day (day 1) and feed them on the last day when we get back to the car (day 6).

A 14-Day Trip For 2 Plus 2 Dogs

how much weight? Since there are only 2 (experienced) adults, our basic packs, including inflatable raft and fishing gear, will weigh an already heavy 35 pounds. Add a pound of food per person per day. Add 4 pounds of dog food (out of 7) which we'll carry during the off-trail part of the trip. Total pack weight: 50 pounds. Too heavy! But our route takes us on a loop, so we'll stash about 10 pounds of food (6 of ours, 4 of the dogs') in a cache on day 2 (see "Caching Food," below). That drops us to 45 pounds, and as the dogs' food is consumed, they can carry weight from our packs until we pick up the cache.

dietary considerations? We've traveled together so often that individual preferences have long since blended into an undifferentiated "backpackers' taste."

fishing prospects? Good to excellent. We're familiar with the area, though not with 2 of the 3 lakes on our itinerary, which are reputed to be great: no trail access and lots of 12-inch brook trout. We know the third lake has no trail, steep, deep banks, and rainbow and brook trout.

The raft will help there. As things worked out, the unfamiliar lakes had new and clearly marked trails to them, were overpopulated (a whole Boy Scout troop showed up on a day trip) and the smaller lake was too shallow for fish. But the bigger lake gave us all we wanted: not quite the reputed 12-inchers, but good eating anyway. The familiar lake neither disappointed nor surprised. We worked hard and ate fish every day, sometimes twice. If the fishing had failed we might've had to leave a couple of days early. We were prepared for it, so there'd be no hard feelings toward the lake, the fish, or ourselves.

fires permitted? Yes, with a permit. Wood is accessible, so we could go minus a stove and fuel.

how many hot meals? We plan on 1 a day for 12 days. We also plan a lot of baking. Plentiful fishing actually meant 2 hot meals many days. By the time we walked out, we'd used up all our supplies, giving our last salami and cheese to an old-timer on the trail who was running low. In retrospect, the fish made us look like planning geniuses: no wasted or surplus food.

FOOD FOR A 14-DAY, 2-PERSON TRIP		
Staples	Pounds	Ounces
18 eggs	2	4
3 sticks margarine		12
Cooking oil		12
Maple Syrup		12
Sugar		12
Baking goods	4	
Beans, rice, onions, garlic	2	8
Spices, condiments	1	
Subtotal	12	12
Ready To Eat		
Salami, cheese, jerky	3	8
Soups		8
Swiss Miss chocolate drink	1	
Tiger's Milk Bars, chocolate	2	8
Cookies and crackers	2	
Dried fruits and nuts	3	
Brandy		12
Subtotal	13	12
*TOTAL NET WEIGHT***	26	
** Dog food for 2 dogs, 12 days 18 lbs.		

An 8-Day Trip For 6 People

how much weight? Six adults, 5 of whom can carry full weight. The 6th has a weak back and can carry no more than 25 pounds under optimum conditions. The weight in food alone for this many people and days (1½ pounds per person per day, for a total of 72 pounds) is so great that sacrifices must be made in other areas. The raft stays home. So does the fry pan, the cooking oil and a lot of liquid condiments. Five people will carry average packs of 44 pounds (3O lbs. in basic weight, 14 lbs. of food); one carries a lightened basic pack of 25 pounds. "Average" packs are, of course, abstractions. Some people are bigger or taller than others or more experienced, more self-sacrificing or just more fanatical. So pack weights will vary. As it turned out, Rick and Hal carried the heaviest packs. Claire, Bryan and Polly, all irrepressible first-timers, carried roughly equal (and heavy) packs, and Karen of the ailing back stuck carefully to her weight limit. No dogs on this trip.

dietary considerations? Claire and Bryan are from England and insist on lots of tea. Everything else is quickly agreed on, a miracle with 6 people. Claire's aversion to mung beans (in her Dorset dialect, "Och, the moong beans!") surfaced 4 days into the trip, as did Polly's closet addiction to the cookies: no problems adjusting.

fishing prospects? Excellent. We're going to a remote lake a day's cross-country trek from the trail, filled with 15-inch Golden Trout, savvy but catchable as we know from previous visits. In fact, the fishing was a disaster. Unaccountably, there were no bugs on the water at all. This made for a comfortable campsite but hardly any fish. Nothing worked: lures, flies, grasshoppers, salmon eggs. We finally caught three during a rainstorm, and that was all.

fires permitted? Not above 10,000 feet. We'll need the stove and fuel for 2 days' use above that altitude.

how many hot meals? One a day will suffice. Plus lots of baking on the 3 days planned in camp. This is a long trip. It will take 3½ days of walking to get in, another day and a half to get out. That calls for less elaborate meals. In fact, with so many people, we decide dinner menus are necessary, especially when we'll be cooking on the stove. Seven dinners are planned; we won't need one our last day.

DINNER MENUS:

Day 1: Turkey (jerky) and rice casserole
Day 2: Cheese and rice souffle
Day 3: Hot vichysoisse (leek soup with dehydrated potatoes)*
Day 4: Macaroni and cheese

FOOD FOR AN 8-DAY, 6-PERSON TRIP

Staples	Pounds	Ounces
2 doz. eggs	2	13½
4 sticks margarine	1	
Rice	3	2
Beans	1	8
Macaroni	2	8
Mung Beans	1	
Flour	4	8
Cornmeal	1	6½
Yeast and baking powder		12
Sugar	2	8
Powdered milk		12
Garlic and dried onion		8
Spices and condiments		11
Subtotal	23	1 2/5

Ready To Eat		
2 Italian salamis	2	5
Assorted cheeses	8	
Dried fruits	7	
Nuts	5	
Dried Meats/jerky	2	
Dried vegetables	1	
Granola	1	3
Tiger's Milk Bars, chocolate	5	
Cookies	6	
Crackers	3	
Swiss Miss	3	
Tea and coffee		12
Instant Oatmeal		13
Dried soups	1	
Raisins	1	
Brandy	1	
Subtotal	48	1
TOTAL NET WEIGHT	71	2½

Day 5: Baked trout and rice (black bean soup if no trout)
Day 6: Rice and bean pudding
Day 7: Minestrone soup*
 *cooked on campstove

We didn't stick precisely to these menus, but with improvisation and the idiosyncrasies of the particular cook on any given day, we managed to consume most of the ingredients we brought along.

Aside from the cruel lack of fish, two other unforseeable conditions also changed our eating plans. Karen became ill late on the first day and we had to spend most of day 2 in camp. This led to hot brunch all around, bland soup for the patient, a late afternoon start, a drastically shortened hike, and a light, though still hot, supper. The other condition was Claire and Bryan's genetic requirement for hot tea each morning and a little warm breakfast before hiking (a boiled egg sufficed) to aid Karen's complete recovery. This used a little more fuel than expected, but was worth it in daily contentment and energy on the uphill legs of the journey. Most important, no one minded that little extra time and work to get warm food and drink into the neediest cases.

Among the items that emerged from our high altitude bakery came corn bread, banana date cake, two chocolate cakes, Karen's fabled mountain challah, and a quiche.

Cooking And Eating Utensils: What We Bring

Spartan backpackers hell-bent for distance can make do with a pot and a spoon. Add a pocket knife to skin a bear or fell a tree and they are content and at peace with the world. Cooking in the wilderness, after all, is no exercise in elegance. However, if you prefer Athens to Sparta, you may want to add just a couple more pots and maybe even a fry pan. The goal is to keep things few and light, but as you'll see from our recipes (Ch. 7), it's possible to satisfy most hedonistic impulses with a minimum of hardware. Here's what we take for 2-8 people on our longer trips.

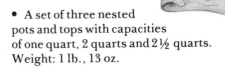

• A set of three nested pots and tops with capacities of one quart, 2 quarts and 2½ quarts. Weight: 1 lb., 13 oz.

• A flex-grip metal pot holder, a pliers-like tool that grips the rim of a pot, one tong fitting under the lip of the rim, the other fitting over it. Weight: 2 oz.

• An 8½-inch teflon-coated aluminum fry pan. It's old enough so that we don't worry about scratching the surface. Otherwise, use a spatula made of wood or plastic instead of metal. A teflon-coated pan requires less shortening, saving weight in the cooking oil department. And it's easy to clean in case of burning on uneven heat. Weight: 1 pound.

• A small aluminum spatula. Weight: 3 oz.

• A plastic egg container (one dozen). Weight: 5½ oz.

• Pocket knives, one each person. We use Tinker model Swiss Army knives, which substitute a Phillips screwdriver for the more common corkscrew. Weight: 3 oz.

• Two small plastic garbage bags for packing the pots and fry pan—for soot containment.

• Two boxes of sulphur kitchen matches packed separately in water-tight Ziploc bags. Weight: 4 oz. (both boxes).

• A small wire whisk. Weight: 3 oz. Alternatively, a small spring-loaded swizzle stick (like an egg-beater). Weight: 3½ oz.

- Eating utensils: 1 Sierra cup (3½ oz.), 1 tin plate (3½ oz.), 1 fork (1½ oz.), and 1 spoon (1½ oz.) per person. The forks are optional; chopsticks are lighter. The pocket knife completes the set.

- Extra Ziploc bags for food storage: Weight: 1 oz.

- An Optimus 323 Purist 1 white gas stove. Weight: 1 lb., 12 oz. Plus 1 liter fuel container (6 oz.) and funnel (1 oz). Alternatively, a Bleuet S200 camping stove plus one butane cartridge. Weight: 1 lb., 7½ oz. These are only taken if necessary.

The total weight (not including the stove equipment) is 5 lb., 14 oz. The Optimus stove and its accessories add 2 lb, 3 oz., for a grand total of 8 lb., 1 oz. Clearly there are expendable items here. Consider how much time you want to spend, and what kind of cooking you plan to do. Then adjust the utensils accordingly.

Shopping

Light And Quick Foods

In the above trip plans, freeze-dried foods are conspicuous by their absence. After many years of sampling, we found we didn't really like or need them. First and foremost, our budget never allowed it—freeze-dried foods aren't cheap. Second, we don't like their taste. Between lumps of undissolved powder and bland seasonings, they often convey the grim message, "Don't eat me." Third, we don't need their convenience. With a fire, our rice, beans and dried veggies do just fine. Where a stove is required, minute rice, soups and noodles work as well and are a lot cheaper.

Nevertheless, freeze-dried foods *are* remarkably convenient. Light in both bulk and weight, they're quick and easy to prepare. Supermarkets carry some, but the largest selections are found in camping or specialty stores. (To order by mail, see "Appendix.") And many people find them quite palatable. The enthusiastic claim by Thomas Winnett, one of the most respected and widely read backcountry authors, that some freeze-dried dinners are good enough to serve guests at home, probably says more about Winnett's taste buds than about truth in advertising.

Bulk Foods

Far superior to freeze-dried are bulk foods—rice, beans, pasta, lentils and peas, nuts, raisins, dried fruits. They're cheaper than packaged varieties, are bought in just the weights you want, rather than what the processor wants to sell you, and exist in enough varieties to satisfy just about everyone. Brown sugar, brown rice, rye or soy flour, 57 varieties of noodles—most bulk food stores have what you need.

Alternative Foods

A world of other possibilities exists out there in the market place. One friend, after spending nearly ten years as a reporter in Tokyo, relies almost exclusively on Japanese food products. He takes Japanese noodles (*soba*); he also carries seaweed (*nori*) which he wraps together in a flexible bamboo square used in rolling rice for Japanese *sushi* (raw fish and rice delicacy). He also relies on soy bean soup bases (*miso*), dried fish, and, unaccountably, popcorn. Others carry falafel mix, a practical and delicious Middle Eastern grain and chick pea combination. And for the sentimental mid-Americanist, there are always instant mashed potatoes and Rice-a-roni.

Extravagances

If backpacking were a science, there'd be no room for frills. We'd have to leave fresh eggs at home, along with mustard powder and sesame oil. But backpacking's an art, subject to (some) whim and a (little) fancy, and that allows for incorporation of particular idiosyncrasies into the overall weight limit. If you absolutely cannot do without some Granny Smith apples, or a watermelon, pare down the weight elsewhere. Your extravagance becomes a working part of your inventory. You have turned a frill into a necessity.

Dog Food

Dry dog food is too bulky to take on a mountain trip; canned dog food is full of water *and* prohibitively expensive. That leaves moist dog food, which is not as bulky as the dry, nor quite as expensive or heavy as the canned, and, according to the makers' claims, more nutritional per unit of weight. It's also conveniently packaged. We always allow our pooches a little more than the minimum requirements, but never so much that they can't carry most of it. For our (medium-sized) dogs, 6 packets are sufficient for a 4 day trip, 10 packets for a 7 day trip. The only other thing to remember is that dogs, like humans, can carry only so much weight. Make appropriate allowances for your dog's size.

Weighing, Packing, Transporting And Caching Food

Weighing Food

Virgil, a fanatical solo backpacker who goes out for 6 weeks at a time without resupplying, refuses to weigh his food. He just eyeballs the amount, tests the "feel" of his pack, and goes off. He hasn't starved or expired of muscle fatigue yet. The rest of us mortals need reassurance that we have the right amount of food for the finite number of days we'll be on the trail. It need not be exact. If you've gone rigid with anxiety over our fine-tuned weighing in those food lists above, relax. You needn't be a charter member of the U.S. Bureau of Standards to backpack. The important number is the total weight—that's what you'll carry. To determine this, a bathroom scale will work just fine.

When you get the food home from the market, eliminate all extraneous packaging. The aim is to get as close to the net weight as possible without sacrificing freshness or, where necessary, protection against breakage. You may want to keep the RyKrisp in its cardboard box to prevent crumbling, the soup powder in its packet to save cooking instructions, or the Tiger's Milk Bars in their aluminum wrappers for protection against the sun. But as a rule, repack almost everything in plastic bags. Then fetch the bathroom scale. Weigh yourself. Now weigh yourself holding all the food in a cardboard box or brown paper bag. Don't forget the eggs, cheese, salami and other things stashed in the fridge. You won't be able to read the scale because the food box will be in the way. Ask a friend to read it for you. That's what friends are for. You now have an idea of the total net weight. If it much exceeds your expectations (1½-2 pounds per person per day), start cutting and paring. Some of the flour can go; put some of the maple syrup back in the cupboard; on second thought, who needs that many almonds? Now get back on the scale. If you're a couple pounds over or under, it's close enough. When you reach the trailhead, you can cut or add again.

*Have a very close friend
read the scale...*

If you own a small postal scale, the kind that weighs packages up to about 4 pounds, you can fine tune by weighing individual items. And if you're a classic anal compulsive, you can even get a letter scale that is calibrated to half-ounces. That way you can be content in the knowledge that exactly 3½ ounces of cinnamon and sugar are nestled against the 1½ ounces of nutmeg and cloves. Authors of backpacking books somehow always feel obliged to know such things; no one else we've ever met on the trail has known or cared.

Packing And Transporting Food

Don't knock plastic. The Ziploc bag just may be the most important advance in backpacking since the invention of the foot. We sympathize with those who hate Ziplocs; we often can't get them closed either. If you're a Zipophobe, pack your food in sturdy plastic bags and secure them with wire ties. If you can deal with Ziploc technology, buy several boxes and use them liberally. So liberally in fact, that you'll double-bag many items.

Individual foods should be packed separately. Cookies, nuts, dried fruit, etc., get packed in their own bags. Liquids such as syrups and oils should be kept in well-sealed containers and carried upright. Don't put them upright in your pack and then lay it on its side for a 5-hour drive to the trailhead; you may find a syrup-soaked pack when you arrive. Pack liquids upright in a box in the car and transfer them to the pack before you start to hike.

Eggs should be packed in plastic containers you can buy at camping stores. They come in half-dozen and dozen sizes and keep the eggs from breaking even if the pack gets dropped or slammed around. Some people prefer to pack breakfast, lunch and dinner foods separately, each in their own section of the pack. Others, like ourselves, prefer to organize the staples apart from the ready-to-eat (trail) foods. Whichever system you use, what's important is that it works for you.

In the off-season, collect plastic bottles. Small ones are perfect for vinegar, sesame oil and hot sauce; large ones for cooking oil, maple syrup and brandy. Compartmentalized pill boxes, obtainable in drug stores, are great for carrying spices. On the trail, carry extra plastic bags. They'll come in handy to replace torn ones, or for caught fish, map cases and garbage bags.

Once everything is swathed in plastic or secured in containers and bags, you need to get it into the packs. It's common to pack at home and transport the filled packs in your car to the trailhead. But loaded backpacks take up lots of space in a car. Especially if you drive a compact, you could leave the final packing for the trailhead and transport the food in boxes and a cooler (for the perishables). Then tie the empty backpacks on the roofrack.

Be sure you know where in the pack your food is. If you dive in after gorp and cheese for lunch and can only come out with cornmeal, you might be nettled. So do a little planning. Someone might carry the lunch foods; someone else the staples, liquids, and dinners. If you're a large party, 2 people can carry the ready-to-eats and 2 the staples. Within any pack, try to be consistent, so nuts and raisins are in the same place every day and are not crushed by an onslaught of cheese. And while in camp, where most cooking, baking and eating are going on, system becomes crucial. We try to arrange the packs in camp so all the baking gear is in one place, all the condiments and spices in another, the jerky, salami, cheese and crackers in the left upper pocket, the chocolate in the fridge, the cookies in the cupboard, and so on. If 2 packs will accommodate all the food in camp, it becomes more efficient. Only those 2 packs have to be moved periodically to keep up with the shade.

Caching Food

We'd never made a food cache until we met an old-timer a year or so ago who convinced us that it was easy and efficient. The simplicity was at first unbelievable. He took the food he wanted to stash, stored it in plastic containers stuffed in a green plastic garbage bag and thrown on the floor of the forest. Nothing more. He insisted that bears and other cognoscenti rarely disturbed the sack and when they did, they never got through the plastic. Were we being taken? We'll probably never know, because we take a few more precautions with our own cache. Old coffee cans and plastic half-gallon ice cream containers with tight lids make up our inner defenses, in which we pack and tightly seal 10 pounds of extra food. We then stuff them in a garbage bag, and bury the stash under a canopy of rocks under a low-spreading tree high in a mountain meadow. We've never retrieved the cache in less than perfect condition.

A couple of hints. Store relatively dispensable food: dog food, supplementary sweets. Make sure the cache is out of the sun. Make even surer you can find it again. That particular tree might not look so particular from a mile away. Or the meadow may be shin-deep in water when you get back and look very different from your last view. Sight your cache from different angles. You don't need a compass, just a sense of proportion and a good memory.

Allow space in your pack for the cache food and its large containers when you leave the trailhead. You may have to hang the empty containers from your pack until you get to the cache site, or stow them in the pack already filled, if there's space. Finally, grin and bear it if the bears or squirrels get what you've squirreled away. It's not that awful to hike out a day or 2 early. Besides, you may catch enough extra fish to compensate for your losses.

PART TWO:

Getting There

CHAPTER IV:
Hiking, Maps & Trails

Packing Your Pack

We usually arrive at the trailhead late at night. We crawl into our sleeping bags, and the next thing we know, the sun is coming up—it's time to hit the trail. Half awake, we squint mournfully at the little Datsun station wagon that brought the 4 of us here. The seats are piled with coats and parkas, the back is full of food boxes, and strapped to the roof rack is a monstrous heap of packs, ponchos, and stuffsacks. How will we ever fit all that gear into our packs? And how much can we possibly pack into the backcountry on our backs?

Everything seems so disorganized the first morning that it's a miracle when we square things away. But somehow it all fits into the packs, and somehow we contrive to pack it into the mountains. We just keep telling ourselves that the packs are always heaviest and the hike always hardest this first morning. And each day, as we hike farther into the wilderness, the load gets lighter, our bodies get stronger, and the packing gets easier.

How should you pack a backpack? First decide what you'll need during the day. What does the weather look like? Will you need easy access to rain ponchos and plastic bags to cover the packs? Or will you want to change into shorts at midday? Change of clothes, along with sunglasses, suntan lotion, maps, candy bars, and other small essentials need to be within easy reach. Lunch and munch food should also be easily accessible. Plan to take pictures at every scenic point? If so, keep your camera in a handy pouch.

After the small, reachable pockets have been filled, the main compartments can be packed. It may sound obvious, but keep in mind that whatever goes into the pack first will come out last. Also, heavy items should go next to your back and as high in the pack (between shoulders and waist) as you can get them. That means the pots and pans, stove and fuel go in first. Heavy food packages, such as flour, rice and beans, go next. That two pound block of cheddar cheese (less some for lunch) falls in the ''heavy'' category too, as does Charles Dickens.

Once those are packed, separate the rest by function. We usually make one compartment the ''drug store/emergency room.'' Another is the ''hardware/fix-it shop.'' You might designate a ''candy store'' as well. Save the lightest items—ponchos and ensolite pads—to strap onto the top of the packs.

Organizing by function lends itself to packing as a group. One person may have the cheese, another the utensils and spices, and a third might end up with 2 sleeping bags and an inflatable raft. One person could be responsible for all liquid containers: cooking oil, maple syrup, vinegar, etc.; make sure this pack always stays upright. No one carries more than he or she feels capable of. And if a shoulder or neck begins to ache after 2 miles, we reorganize, trading a heavy sleeping bag for a lighter ensolite pad.

There's room to strap things on the top and bottom of most packs; a stuffed sleeping bag, rolled-up poncho, tent, or stuffsack full of clothes, items easy to trade if one person's pack is too much for weak knees or a bad back. But be careful. A rule of thumb is that anything hanging below your waist ''feels'' about 50 percent heavier than it would up next to the middle of your back. Anything strapped to the top of the pack feels about 75 percent heavier than it really is. And whatever hangs behind you in the middle of the pack gains a good 100 percent because it is so far behind, swinging as you walk.

When strapping on pads, tents and stuffsacks, it's important to double-knot everything. Tie each stuffsack pullcord in a double-bow. Each strap gets wrapped back around itself, then knotted. Never leave anything that might work loose as you hike. This is especially important if you're the last person in line. We've had a few instances where things fell out of stuffsacks or off packs, but usually the person immediately behind noticed. If you're last, the wool sweater you drop will probably stay lost. And when you're shivering at night, you'll become a life-long convert to the double knot.

A couple other tips from the school of hard knocks. Don't keep your maps or permits in your pants pockets. They'll invariably get wet from sweat, fog or rain. Once that happens, and the colors and lines start to run together, they become difficult to use at all. In fact, most books recommend keeping maps in a plastic bag inside the pack so they won't get wet in a sudden downpour (or if they're below a cracked bottle of vinegar, a leaky tube of suntan oil or a broken egg).

If the weather's been wet, try to keep the waterlogged rainflies and ponchos separate from the tents and sleeping bags when heading out the next day. The tents and sleeping bags may be damp in the morning, but they won't be nearly as wet as the rainflies. Pack them separately, even if it means breaking up a logical pair, such as tent-and-rainfly or sleeping-bag-and-ground-cloth. You need not pack every-

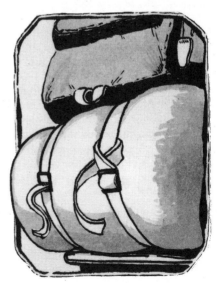

Wrap the strap back around itself into a knot

thing in the same manner each day, or even from morning to afternoon. Also, remember that your backpack is a natural drying platform. Wet socks? Dripping poncho? Hang them securely from the pack as you hike, rotate them occasionally to get the sun on all sides, and by the end of the day, they'll be dry.

Finally, your belt or belt loops can act as an extension of your pack. Lots of backpackers loop a Sierra cup over their belts, ready for a quick, cool drink at a stream without having to take off their packs or go through contortions to get the head down to the water. And don't forget to secure things on your belt—cups, knives, gorp pouches—with the same care you take with things hanging off your pack.

Adjusting The Pack To You

Three things connect you to the pack: 2 shoulder straps and a hip strap. All 3 should be padded; unpadded ones tend to cut into clothes or skin. It's best to have someone help you with the initial adjustment of the straps. Then, when they're right, you might want to put a safety pin or knot in the straps to prevent their slipping as you walk.

Adjust the hip belt first, with someone holding the pack against your back. The belt should rest on your hip bones tightly enough to hold the pack there. Then, tighten the shoulder straps so the pack is held upright but doesn't pull on your shoulders. The pack should actually ride on your hips, which support most of the weight. The shoulder straps are meant to take very little weight; they mainly keep the pack in position, straight up and centered over your hips.

As you hike, the pack should not cut into your back. Sometimes a misplaced belt buckle or stove piece will protrude and become a pain. Sometimes shoulder straps cut into shoulder bones. They can usually be shifted sideways to get a better fit and temporary relief. Also, the spots on each hip where the pack makes contact might get a little sore.

Occasionally you'll want to shift weight to rest your hips. Simply loosen or release your hip belt. The pack will drop about an inch, your shoulder straps will

tighten and the weight will now be on your shoulders. Experiment as you walk—more weight on the hips or shoulders—until you find the right distribution. After a day or so, pack, back, and hips all seem to mesh comfortably into an incredible walking machine.

Tips On Getting Acclimated

The week before your trip, you run around like the proverbial headless chicken, lists in hand, trying to arrange every detail while working an 8 hour day. You're up half the last night trying to finish packing. You leave early the next morning, drive hours to the trailhead and immediately begin to hike. You're at 5,000 feet, walking uphill, with the pack at its maximum weight. Your body is not accustomed to so much strain; all day you feel dizzy, nauseous, achey. That night your brain feels like it's trying to come out of your ears. You're camped at a beautiful lake at the top of the world, and all you want to do is crawl headfirst into your sleeping bag until the pain goes away.

This isn't inevitable; it needn't happen to you. With a little forethought and a few precautions, you can avoid Early Trip Discomfort (ETD). Here's how:

- Even if you have only a week for your trip, plan a whole day to drive to and sleep at the trailhead. That first night in the thin air will help acclimate your body to the first hard day on the trail.
- Eat breakfast. Anything which gives you protein, fat, and carbohydrate is adequate. Cheese and crackers, a granola bar, or peanut butter and jelly make a fine start. Most of your initial hiking will usually be over by early afternoon, so breakfast is the main source of energy for the day's challenges.
- You might want to use salt and aspirin.(This applies only to people not adversely affected by either of these substances. Salt can cause nausea; aspirin can upset the stomach.) The salt can be in food, such as salami, jerky or crackers. Some people take it in pill form or direct from the container. We also often take one or 2 aspirin first thing on the morning of a long hike.
- Start early. This is hard for the leisurely-breakfast junkies, but that's invariably the most pleasant time to hike. The cool air is refreshing and you don't lose a lot of water through sweating. The sun isn't blinding, the rocks aren't hot, and by the time the afternoon thundershowers begin you've arrived at your destination and set up camp.
- Wear sunglasses and a hat or visor. You've heard of snow blindness, caused by the intense glare of the sun off a white snowfield. The

same problems can be caused by reflections of sunlight from grey granite boulder fields. The mountain air is thin and the mountain sun is bright. Work on your face tan once you're in camp. While hiking, it's better to keep your eyes and face covered, especially for the first few days.

- Drink plenty of water. Stop on the trail when you get thirsty. Drink a few cups before the steep uphill climb. We carry a minimum quart of water for every 2 people, but it's not a bad idea to start with even more. You can always pour it out if you're sure that the streams you expect to cross are running full. Several times we planned to fill the canteens at a stream which was running on the map but dry as a bone on the trail. That meant several miles of dry throats. In the spring, there's water everywhere. In the fall, however, be careful. Extra water is heavy, but it's much more uncomfortable to hike when you're thirsty.

- Don't be afraid to stop and rest, or vary your pace, which often accomplishes the same thing. The destination is rarely over that next rise. A steady slow pace will get you there with fewer problems and less pain than the sprint-and-collapse method. Remember the tortoise and the hare.

- Keep the carbohydrates coming. Stop for energy food about mid-morning, or carry a pouch of gorp to munch as you hike. We like chocolate and Tiger's Milk Bars; crackers and jelly work as well. Sweets give you that instant pick-up you can use along the trail. If you know your limits and don't push too far beyond them, and if you're not afraid to stop and relax, you'll do just fine. Two days into the trip, you'll be hiking farther, breathing easier, resting as often as you like without fear that you won't get "There," and carbo-loading like a champ.

Crossing Streams

Many trails are constructed so that horses, not people, can cross streams. The trail crosses a stream at a level, wide area with a rocky bottom. A horse doesn't care if there are stepping stones. A horse also doesn't care if the water is one or 5 feet deep. Unfortunately, it's not as easy for a human to wade across in 3 feet of freezing, rushing water. A stream is always a wise place to take a break. Make it a point to ponder before you ford. Make it another point to scout the stream up and down for the best crossing.

One spring Rick and a friend, Saginaw Sam, were among the first backpackers on the trail after a wet winter. About halfway to their destination, they came to a stream running high, fast and cold. Sam, a first-time backpacker, took one look and decided that wading was not part of the contract. They negotiated a compromise. Rick would wade across with both packs, one at a time. Sam would head a few yards upstream to a stretch of water which was deeper, but strewn with enough high boulders to let him step across. Sam balanced gingerly on the first boulder. He hopped to the next, then the third. Two more to go. The second-to-last boulder was unsteady. So was Sam. With arms flailing and eyes wide, he plunged into the foaming torrent. Luckily he only got a few bruises and soaked clothing. Had he decided to boulder-hop with his pack on—including his sleeping bag and all his extra clothes—it would have been a lot worse.

Late in the summer, when there's not much water flowing, you can hop from boulder to boulder without much trouble or danger of getting everything wet. But early in the spring, it's better to wade. So you have to get wet. It's that simple.

Well, hopefully it's that simple. A pair of sneakers or tennies, which you've brought along to use in camp, come in handy here. The water is usually so glacial and the bottom of the stream so rocky, that going barefoot is painful and dangerous. Just remove your socks, sling your boots around your neck, don the Converse and head in. If you didn't bring any sneakers, wear your boots, sans socks. Once across, drain your boots and put on a pair of dry socks, which will soak up most of the moisture as you hike on. At your next rest break, change into a second pair of dry socks, and by the time you get to camp your boots will be dry.

During the spring, the level of a stream rises noticeably during the day as the sun melts snowfields high above, and falls again each night as snow refreezes after sundown. The best time to cross a stream is early in the morning; the worst time is late in the afternoon.

Be especially careful of stream depth: *do not* confuse clear water with shallow. Mountain streams are often so crystal clear that what looks like a 2-foot bottom might actually be 6 feet deep. It's a good idea to cross once without a pack to be sure you can make it without encountering any dangerous flows or depths. It's much easier to bail out and turn back with nothing weighing you down. Caution is the key.

It helps to carry a big stick or wading staff when crossing. You can distribute weight more evenly on 3 points than on 2. As long as you walk slowly and carefully, with the staff downstream, and don't mind numb feet and legs, you'll get across safe and sound.

What about using a rope? It's possible, of course, and sometimes necessary. But our own rule of thumb is: if a crossing is so dangerous that it *requires* using a rope, don't do it unless it's *more* dangerous to stay where you are. In an emergency, a 2-person party with about 150 feet of 5-millimeter climbing rope can ford a stream like this:

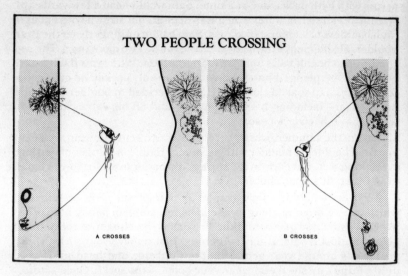

TWO PEOPLE CROSSING

A CROSSES

B CROSSES

Step one. The rope is tied to a tree, wrapped once around the forder, then held by the anchor-person who stands downstream of the forder and pays out rope from the coil. The anchor person is *not* tied to the rope. The forder always faces upstream while crossing. If s/he falls, the anchor-person hauls her/him in. Once across, the forder waits while the anchor-person unties the rope from the tree. The length of free rope is then hauled over and tied to a tree on the far side. Step two. The rope extends from the tree to the original anchor-person, who wraps it once around the waist and then tosses the remaining coil to the first forder. First forder walks downstream of the second forder and pulls in slack as the second forder, also facing upstream, makes her/his way across.

It may take 2 trips to get a single backpack load across a stream, because the stuff sacks which hang from the pack can't be left in place if the water is deeper than about 2 feet. When you're wading with a pack on, it's advisable to unbuckle the hip strap. That way, if you fall, you can release the pack easily and not get swept under or downstream by it. Once you've safely negotiated the stream and carried all the gear over, dry off, take another rest, repack, put the return crossing out of mind, and head up the trail.

If a log happens to be across the stream just where you want it, don't let such luck go to your head. Take your time. Log walking above a rushing stream can feel like walking a tightrope. And like tightrope walkers, you may want to use a long stick or staff as a balance rod. Ideally it should be longer than you are tall, but it doesn't have to be. Hold it even with your waist as you cross the log. Also, beforehand, come to terms with everybody's sense of balance in your party. The surest-footed member should take the packs over. The unsurest should sit, straddle the log and inch across. And if you're traveling with dogs, one of you may have to wade across with them on a leash. We've never been able to persuade our pooches to walk the log.

Summing up, when wading across a stream, 1) wear sneakers or boots but not socks; 2) check depth; 3) use a big branch as a wading staff; 4) face upstream when crossing; 5) unbuckle your hip belt.

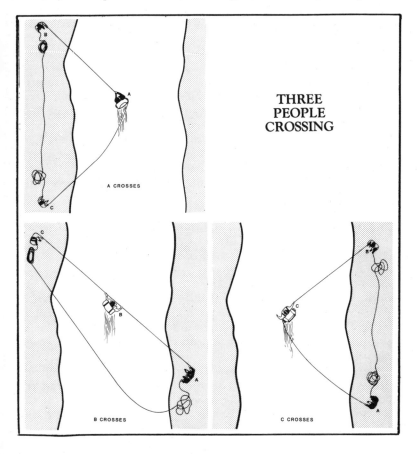

THREE
PEOPLE
CROSSING

A CROSSES

B CROSSES

C CROSSES

Hiking In The Rain

We once made a list of "Things to Do When it Rains," and hiking was at the top. That's because huddling in a tent or under a poncho can get awfully boring, and keeping everything in a campsite dry *without* cramming it all into the tent with you is a practically unattainable goal. If you can keep dry, hiking in the rain is fun, pretty, and actually easier than hiking in very hot conditions.

There are many "systems" for keeping yourself and your pack dry in the rain. We prefer to wear short ponchos designed to cover a person without a pack on. These can be used around camp without dragging in the mud, and while fishing in the rain. The special ponchos designed to cover you and your pack are so long they can be unwieldy. If the weather is warm, a short poncho and a pair of hiking shorts are ideal for a walk in the rain.

There are special backpack covers, but garbage bags are a lot cheaper and just as light. Punch two holes and feed the shoulder straps through before hoisting the pack onto your back. The garbage bags flap a little in the wind, but they keep the pack very dry. Buy the thickest ones you can find and carry an extra or two.

Sometimes there may be no getting away from a prolonged spell of foul weather. However, many summer rains are of the "afternoon thundershowers" variety. They come on fast, last a short time, then move off. Often, the mornings are gorgeous, and at 2:00 p.m. there's not a cloud in the sky. But by 4:00, you find yourself huddled in a forest as the thunder crashes around you and huge hailstones bounce off your head. From the comfort of a cottage a thundershower can be terrific; at 8,000 feet, near the timberline, however, it can be terrifying and dangerous. You need to keep dry and stay safe — if possible among the smaller trees. Easy access to the plastic garbage bag and a poncho will let you stay dry and cover ground at the same time. Or, if you prefer to sit it out, protect your pack while you watch the thunder and lightning roll across the mountain tops. The poncho will keep most of you dry, and while you end up with wet boots, socks, and maybe pants legs, it's rarely enough to worry about.

However, when it rains, beware of hypothermia! It needn't be cold out — even wind and rain at 60 degrees F can make you dangerously chilled. The symptoms are uncontrolled shivering, followed by the inability to think clearly. Don't wait to reach your destination to deal with this. Get out of the wind and your wet clothes. Start a fire or crawl into a protected sleeping bag. Drink something hot. Huddle close to others who are dry. Rest and get warm.

If you're going to an area where it rains hard or for days at a time, this may require serious preparation. "Foul weather gear" (like that used on sailboats), special backpack covers, boot covers, Gore-Tex wool parkas (which ingeniously keep the rain out while letting your sweat escape)—all or some of those things may be necessary. Check out the weather conditions before you leave home. Most backpacking trips, however, are predicated on sunny weather, and wet ponchos or socks can usually be dried out in the warm morning sunshine.

Mud And Snow

From the hillside above, a lush Sierra meadow looks like a golfing green. But trying to hike across it in the first few weeks after snow melt is like trying to run through tapioca. Each step is an effort. Your boots get stuck in the mud. We've known people to lose their boots entirely in the slimy goo, pulling up their feet to find nothing but a sock on. If there's an alternative trail which skirts the springtime meadow, take it. It will save time, physical effort and mental exhaustion. It will also save the ecologically fragile meadowland.

Snow is normally considered a problem for winter backpackers, but it can stay on the ground long into the spring and summer. The trouble is, snow can be hard or soft, icy or slushy, sticky or slippery. It can be a pleasant stroll or a dangerous slide, and you need to be careful on it.

Mornings, snow is usually icy and slick. A very slight gradient can send your feet from under you. Even worse, it might start you sliding down an icy slope into a freezing river or lake. As the day progresses, the snow begins to melt. By late afternoon it may have turned into sticky slush. Like mud, this kind of snow is a disheartening inconvenience. It slows you down but isn't likely to hurt you. Beware, however, of "snow bridges" which may collapse during hot afternoons. A snow bridge is a layer of snow—perhaps a foot or more in depth—over a large hole caused by flowing water (from melted snow) underneath. Step on the bridge in the morning, and it will hold you. Do so in the afternoon and you'll fall through. A likely spot for snow bridges is next to large rocks, which absorb heat and melt snow from below at the same time the sun melts it from above. The result is a sort of ice cavern whose sides are prone to collapse when weight is put on them.

Our advice is try to avoid hiking over more than short stretches of snow. If you must, hike early. When you get to the snow line, don't plan to go much farther; it may be dangerous. If you know in advance that there will be a lot of unmelted snow on the trail, bring a pair of crampons to strap onto your boots. These are spikes which allow you to walk on both icy or slippery snow without much danger of falling. They won't help in very soft, powdery snow, for which you need snowshoes or cross-country skis, but they will get you safely through most springtime snow conditions with a minimum of bruises and sore muscles.

The other thing to consider before you tromp off above the snow line is that firewood up there is probably buried beneath a foot or 2 of wet slush. That makes cooking and warming a great deal more time-consuming and complicated.

Dealing With Fears And Phobias

As we noted earlier, you take all of yourself into the mountains when you go backpacking. It's impossible to leave the bad parts behind. This means that your whole party has to deal with anyone's particular hang-ups, and you should know what they are before you go. But you should *not* let them stop you from going. Hal, for example, is scared of heights. Really scared. He learned it to his surprise about 12 years ago when he was half-way up a Mayan temple pyramid in the Yucatan. Convinced that he was about to pitch backwards into space, he clung for dear life to the safety chain, inched to the top, sat down in a cold sweat, fantasized helicopter rescues and other humiliations, and eventually invented one of mountaineering's newest and most useful (if less graceful) techniques: "rappaporting."

Rappaporting is a play on the word "rapelling" and has nothing in common with it. To rappaport is to get from Point A to Point B *very carefully*. Any way you can, do it. It usually involves a good bit of frantic caution, inelegant clambering, and the use of the "sidle," as you inch your bottom and those jellied appendages called legs over the loose shale toward the haven of a firm root or branch or a six-million year-old boulder. You can tell you're rappaporting when other members of the party, no more experienced than you, move confidently, even nimbly, on 2 sure feet over the same terrifying terrain.

In short, it's perfectly possible to live with a fear of heights in the mountains and enjoy the trip thoroughly. It's okay to laugh *with* the person who makes fun of his or her own phobia. It's *not* okay to laugh at them. A foreknowledge of the problem, a helping hand, plus a whole lot of support and common sense gets one through.

The same is true in camp. One of our friends has a deep abiding fear of spiders. It means taking extra care that tent flaps and mosquito nettings are *always* tightly secured. And it means doing a careful spider search for that friend whenever the request is made. A little extra effort and support makes backpacking both possible and fun for someone whose fears might otherwise preclude it.

Support for somebody's fears doesn't mean going gooey with concern or "manly" with false bravery. The person who is scared of heights more often than not doesn't need your hand, just a little more time. And the person who's scared of the dark or of mountain thunder doesn't need to be surrounded by firm shoulders to rest on. Unaffected presence is usually enough. In any case, let people know before you set out what may bother you; and let other people know also that it's all right to have their own bothers.

Mosquitos

In late spring, mosquitos can literally drive a hiker crazy. It's not so bad when you're camped—you can escape into your tent and close it up. But when you're hiking through a meadow with a cloud of mosquitos buzzing around your ears and eyes—and sometimes up your nose or into your mouth—you will devoutly wish to be anywhere else on earth. Repellents—such as Cutter's or one of the war-surplus "jungle juices"—will stop the little critters from biting, but it's the humming and buzzing that makes you want to throw yourself off the nearest cliff. Rest stops are pure purgatory, and it's not unusual for you to hike twice as fast and far as planned on total insane energy.

Two suggestions besides the repellent: mosquitos like grass, forest, water, and deep shade. So when you stop to rest, pick a spot as

high, barren, rocky, and windy as you can find. Second, if you hear rumors in advance of a particularly bad mosquito plague in the area you're headed for, you can get lightweight mosquito-net hats which drop a circular netting from a round hat to your shoulders. This will keep the mind-wrenching buzzing away from your ears, eyes, and nose. A long-sleeved shirt and some repellent on your clothes will allow you to hike through even the worst mosquito-infested marshes.

Maps

In Chapter 2 we showed you how to obtain up-to-date Forest and Park Service maps and topographical maps. The first kind, which show distance and direction but not elevation, are fairly easy to read. Trails are marked by broken lines, roads by unbroken lines, unimproved dirt roads by double hash marks, marshes by grass clusters—that sort of thing. The symbols are standardized and you can learn them fast. Best of all, the symbols lie on a flat plane surface (hence the technical name of the maps: planimetric) and are easy to locate and follow. Topographical maps, which show distance, direction and elevation, require some explanation.

A topographical map ("topo" map) does for the backcountry traveler what a street map does for the urban visitor. It helps in the planning of your trip: what the safest and most convenient route is between the trailhead and final destination, how far you want to hike each day, how high you want to climb, which day trips are possible and which aren't worth the effort, what kind of scenery you're likely to encounter: shale and rocks, long vistas, lakes and streams, high mountain meadows, granite passes.

How To Read A Topo Map

The most noticeable things on a topographical map are the thin brown lines running in circles and arcs and squiggles all over the place. These are contour lines—lines corresponding to a specific elevation above sea level. Here's how they work. Imagine a small island in the ocean. At low tide we might draw a line around the island where the water meets the shore. At high tide we might draw another line around the island. Perhaps high tide is 10 feet above low tide. So we now have 2 contour lines, one drawn at low tide, one 10 feet higher drawn at high tide. Imagine next a super high tide 10 feet above normal high tide. We draw another contour line around the island. And then a fourth, fifth and sixth line each where the water meets the shore if the water level keeps rising at 10-foot intervals.

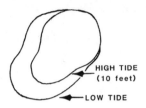

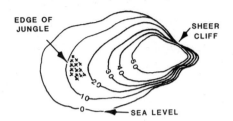

If the lines were large and distinct enough, we could draw the island as it looks from an airplane. Six lines, each representing the shape of the island at a specific height above sea level, would be visible from the air. Now, suppose one side of the island is a sheer 50-foot cliff. All the contour lines will converge on this side when viewed from above, because they are nearly on top of each other. The opposite side of the island might be a wide sandy beach. Our first contour line rings the beach at low tide. Much of the beach is underwater at high tide. So our high tide line (10 feet above sea level) appears far from the first line, nearly at the edge of the jungle. And our line 20 feet above sea level does not touch the beach at all; it's a line through jungle and rocky cliffs.

The lines are widely spaced on the beach area of the island and close together where there are cliffs. This is our first clue to reading topo maps. Two or more lines very close together mean a very steep grade or cliff. Two or more lines wide apart mean a gentle slope or relatively flat area. Thus, for example, a trail that crosses contour lines is a steep trail and one that runs parallel to the lines is level.

Our next illustration (p. 78) is more complicated. There are places where the lines form U's, V's, and figure-eights. Where the contour lines form U's or V's, they indicate either a ridge or a gulley/streambed. A ridge is indicated on the map by a set of U- or V-shaped lines pointing toward lower elevations. A streambed or gulley is marked by a set of U- or V-shaped lines pointing toward higher elevations. On the illustration, our ridge ends in a cliff overlooking the sea, and our streambed/gulley begins high up, at the 60' line, and descends to the sea in a series of inverted V's. Imagine the view from the air. When the 60' line describes an inverted V—facing into the island center—it is traveling along the walls of a streambed. So are the other, lower lines. When the lines describe a V pointing out to sea, they are running along the slopes of a ridge. The figure-eights, observed from above, describe two mountain peaks separated by a fairly gentle slope in one direction (E-W on our illustration) and by fairly steep gulleys in

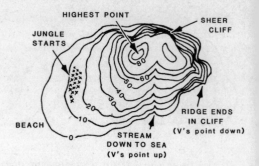

the other direction (N-S). This gives the contours a kind of pinched waist effect which translates into a figure-eight. (If you want some practice reading contour lines, see Bjorn Kjellstrom's *Be Expert with Map and Compass*. He even provides a couple of quizzes.)

The following four simple rules explain the contour lines on a topo map.
- Lines close together means steep gradients.
- Lines farther apart means gentle gradients.
- V-shaped sets of lines pointing to higher elevations means gulleys or streambeds.
- V-shaped sets of lines pointing to lower elevations means ridges.

Scales And Distances

A topographical map has two scales shown at the bottom margin of the map, one indicating distance as the crow flies, one indicating elevation between contour lines. The distance scale is called SCALE, and is represented by a ratio number, such as 1:24000, meaning one inch on the map represents 24000 inches (or 2000 feet) in real linear distance. Under that notation are usually 3 calibrated line figures which represent distance in miles, feet, and kilometers. The elevation scale is called CONTOUR INTERVAL and tells you the vertical distance — elevation — between the contour lines, such as CONTOUR INTERVAL 40 FEET. To make all these squiggles easier to follow, most topographical maps give real elevation readings along darker brown contour lines every hundred or five hundred feet. Thus, for example, 7500 will be marked along a dark brown line. There will then be several light brown contour lines and then another dark brown line with an 8000 on it. You can figure out how hard or easy it'll be to climb up or down those 500 feet by reading the contour lines in between: close together means tough going; far apart, it's a piece of cake. In either case it'll certainly take you longer than walking 500 horizontal feet along a dry meadow. By interpreting distance and elevation readings, you can plan how long and how far you can go in a day.

Topo maps come in different scales. If you see a map with a scale of 1:250000, (one inch equals 20,833 feet), a large distance can be crammed onto it—a whole national park, for example. That's great for a panoramic view of where you are in relation to the rest of the world, but it won't have the kind of detail you want for backpacking. Always try to get the map with the most enlarged detail. Even if you have to carry 2 or 3 high-detail maps to cover the distance you want to go, it'll be worth it. You'll be thankful for all the nooks and crannies, spurs and outcroppings, feeder streams and marshes that such maps foretell.

How To Interpret Map Dates, Colors, And Symbols

Many maps, as we've noted, are outdated. Topo maps, mostly made in the 1950s from aerial photographs, then verified by survey teams, are great on permanent features such as mountains, but often not so great on impermanent roads and trails. Check along the lower border for the date of the map, and if necessary, try to locate a more up-to-date Forest or Park Service map to use in conjunction with it.

The picture from which a topo map is made supposedly was taken in a year of average rainfall during the dry season—late autumn in most parts of the country. The map should show all lakes and rivers at their driest stage. Still, there's no guarantee they'll be the same size or shape when you arrive. Much depends on the season and the latest annual rainfall. When you hike in the spring, that small creek marked on the map by a dotted blue line may be a raging torrent, too tough to cross. That same creek in the fall may be bone dry just when you were planning to stop for some fresh water. Large lakes, rivers, meadows and most physical contours on the map will in fact be just as they're supposed to be. Occasionally a flood or avalanche will have rearranged the topography, but on the whole you can rely on the topo map for contour accuracy.

Maps also show structures visible from the air when the area was photographed. Some are houses, cabins, ranger huts, or run-down old barns. Some may have rotted away completely. Take care not to depend on the topo map to find shelter from a storm: those structures—even bridges—may no longer exist.

Finally, map colors are important. Grey represents treeless, rocky areas. White signifies snow or glacier. Green means forest. Mottled green or green-white shows meadowland. These colors help you hike by describing the terrain. Thus when you plan to leave a marked, manicured trail, it's important to consider not only contour and streams but also the *kind* of terrain you're heading into. A nearly flat manzanita forest is impassable. But the next hillside, while steeper, may be a pine forest crisscrossed with deer trails. Rocky areas are the easiest to cross but may take some climbing to get to. They're found mainly above the treeline at higher altitudes. Some terrain must be analyzed on the spot, but a great deal can be learned from the topo map's colors and symbols.

Trails

A trail is constructed to certain specifications. It must be level across and a certain width. It must have drainage ditches or gutters to channel run-off rain water. Tree branches have to be cleared to a certain height above the trail to allow horseback riders to pass unimpeded. Also, a trail is allowed only a specific angle of inclination. If the grade is too steep, the trail must switch back and forth (hence "switchbacks") so it doesn't exceed the angle at which a horse can comfortably walk up or down. Of course not all trails comply at all points with all rules. But the vast majority of park trails were built with these standards in mind.

Trails are also maintained regularly. Trees are cleared, brush is trimmed, paths are rerouted on a regular basis in areas of flood damage or avalanche. Trail crews are hired to bring the original trail back up to specifications and are paid by the mile. The work is checked by rangers who simply hike the trail behind them, and most parks keep records of trail maintenance. Occasionally a park will abandon a specific trail because it is used so rarely, or to give that particular sector of the backcountry a breather. Sections of an unmaintained trail will disappear almost completely in 3-5 years. If you're planning to take what looks like an "out of the way" trail, it might be a good idea to check that it's being maintained before you begin. Any trail shown on the topo map but not on the more up-to-date Forest Service map should be regarded with suspicion. It may not be there any more.

Don't Cut Corners: They'll Wash Away!

It's difficult to construct switchback trails which won't wash out in the rain. To do this, the trail needs to have drains and run-offs in fixed places. When hikers decide it'll be faster to avoid the switchbacks by going straight up or down the slope, their footsteps tend to dig new drains across the switchbacks. When the rain begins to follow those new, irregular paths downward, the trail quickly erodes. The message, therefore, is clear and simple: when hiking switchbacks, don't cut corners. It'll be easier on your knees and feet to avoid a steep descent with a heavy pack and, more important, it saves the trail for those who come later.

Losing A Trail

Short Cuts

Short cuts are highly unpredictable. The terrain can be tricky or thick with vegetation; there's the danger of getting lost. Short cuts often take longer than the route you're "cutting short."

On one of our first mountain trips we decided to take a short cut. It looked easy on the map: half a mile saved and all downhill. When we started out, we immediately ran into almost impenetrable brush—6-foot high manzanita—solid and prickly. We couldn't see where our feet were landing; we got poked in the eyes. At points it was so steep we had to hang by the nearest branch, then slip and slide our way down. When the grade leveled off, we found ourselves over our heads in bush grass. The going was muddy, hot, slow, frustrating, and just plain dumb. We reached our destination more exhausted and tattered than if we had stuck to the trail. Luckily, we weren't hurt or lost.

Lost And Found

Even if you avoid shortcuts and have the right maps and a compass, it's still not hard to lose a trail. Trail markers may have been destroyed, junctions and turn-offs may be indistinct, or the trail may simply peter out at points. Finely-crafted drainage ditches or dry streambeds might look more like the trail than the trail itself. Deer paths in the woods may seem to be the main one till they cross others that look exactly alike, at which point you begin to wonder where your partners went.

On a recent 4-person trip we found ourselves lagging while our 2 companions wanted to hike faster. It was decided that they'd wait for us at the signpost to "Silver Lake" or at a trail junction. They bounded off without any maps, while we plodded slowly. About an hour later we realized that there'd been neither a sign nor a trail junction, and that we were well beyond Silver Lake. Doubling back, we found the signpost, broken off and obscured by brush, next to the junction which was in an area too rocky and sandy to be seen. Meanwhile we had no idea if our companions had found the lake or not. So Hal sat at the junction with the packs while Rick hiked a mile to the lake, found no one there, and returned. Then Rick sat with the packs while Hal hiked down the main trail until he found our friends drying off after a trailside swim in a tiny lake they assumed was Silver Lake. Soon we were back together, but not without re-learning a couple of lessons: first, never assume trails or crossroads are well-marked or marked at all; and second, never split up in unfamiliar territory.

There are several other things to keep in mind too. The most important is that as long as you have drinking water, food, and the shelter you carry on your back, you can make camp almost anywhere. If you can't find the trail, simply hunker down, take time to mull things over, enjoy your surroundings. Also, never let that pack out of your sight as you wander around in the woods looking for Route 66. And, for that matter, instead of plunging blindly ahead into the unknown, try to back-track; that'll usually return you to square one and get you safely on your way again.

Often even a well-maintained trail can disappear as it crosses granite faces or other rocky terrain. There are no trees with blaze marks or ribbon markers to keep you on course. There are no boot prints in the dust; in fact, there's no dust, only rock. You're standing there without a clue. Go back to where the trail is last visible. Check on your map how far you'll be walking over the rock face. Maybe it doesn't make any difference exactly where you walk if you can key in on your destination, and if the terrain is equally safe in the approximate vicinity of the trail. Above all, look for cairns (sometimes called "trail ducks"): 3 rocks set one on top of the other by some thoughtful hiker who knows the route. They are usually at regular intervals along the rock face or through an open, trackless meadow. Anyone who has ever lost a trail will be grateful to those anonymous friends who took the time to stop and build a cairn.

Other hikers not only sometimes mark the trail, but also often have advice that keeps you on course. Ask lots of questions of those coming from the opposite direction. Where are they coming from? How far is the nearest lake, campsite or watering spot? Where's the best fishing? Does the trail become hard to follow or is it well-marked all the way to your destination? Then *offer* information. Sit down, pull out maps and go over routes. Tell them which way to go. Remind them that a trail marker a mile back was hit by lightning and is no longer visible. They'll be as grateful to you as you are to them.

If, after all your efforts, you can't find a decent, well-marked trail, turn back. You may be on an unmaintained trail. An alternative may have been constructed since your map was made. If you go on, assume that things may get worse and that for all practical purposes you will be doing a "cross-country" — that is, an off-trail — hike.

Off Trail Hiking

Slow and careful are the keys to cross-country or off-trail hiking. Cross-country hiking never happens exactly as planned, and you need plenty of time to stop, figure things out, and rest — off-trail "bushwhacking" tires you faster than on-trail hiking.Give yourself as much time to hike cross-country as you can. To do this, stay on the trail as long as possible before leaving it for the off-trail leg of your trip. Never start out late in the day if you have to be somewhere by nightfall. You might need a whole day to negotiate the rock fall or steep ravine that stands between you and fabled Lake Mooselookmeeguntuk. Reaching your destination is always very slow; the return trip over now familiar terrain will be much faster.

We usually average a 1/4 mile per hour off the trail, and we plan to cover only one or 2 miles in a day. To start as early as possible, we camp near the point where we leave the trail. We *always* lay out our route in advance using the topo map — not difficult for such short daily distances. Just look for a route between 2 points that involves the least change in elevation. Try to avoid places where contour lines run close together. Even if only 2 lines seem to converge, that's a sheer 40 foot cliff — too steep to climb without experience, confidence and the proper gear. Keep the contour lines as far apart as possible when you plan a cross-country trek.

You must be careful with every step when off the trail. You can't let your mind wander to the scenery or to the trout of yesteryear. Eyes must stay on the ground just ahead, checking every footfall. There's lots of balancing to do, especially when hiking through brush. It saps strength, tears stuffsacks, snags fishing rods and anything else not properly battened down on your pack. If you have to go through brush, make sure all ties are double-knotted, all zippers fully zipped. Fishing and tent poles must not stick up above your pack or they will be broken by low-hanging branches. You might fall. In that case fragile objects inside your pack — camera lenses, eggs — may break unless they are properly cushioned.Liquids not tightly contained and encased in plastic will run all over everything.

Keep your hands free to clear brush or grasp at branches to pull yourself along. Mark your route if possible with bits of colored cloth or rope tied to branches so you don't get turned around or lost. And stay together! It's really easy to get separated and lost in thick growth.

Hiking over boulder fields is more common in the high mountains than crashing through brush. It helps to wear hiking boots (rather than tennis or jogging shoes), so the soles are not torn up by walking and balancing on the corners of large boulders. Again, keep your hands free; use them to hold on when you can. Try to test each rock or boulder with light foot pressure before putting all your weight on it. If the rock is wobbly, be careful. It can send you and your 40 pound pack tumbling down a field of granite boulders.

It's generally easier to hike uphill than downhill when you're making your way off the trail. You can plan an uphill route from below, with a good view of the entire hillside. You can't plan a downhill route so easily. Going down, you're likely to come to a steep gradient you couldn't see from above. Suddenly you're staring down at what seems a sheer cliff.

Never assume a straight line is the safest or easiest way from here to there. Use the topo map wisely. Once you figure out the best route try to stick to it closely so long as it proves safe and feels right. The important thing is not to walk yourself into a place you can't return from.

If the going gets too tough, you can stop, turn, or go back. There's no requirement to get anywhere by any time. Never feel pressured to continue even your own pre-planned route. Stay flexible, stay cool, and don't be afraid to change plans and routes. There are other lakes to fish, other streams to camp along, other routes to the same place. There's no need to do something you're afraid of off-trail. Knowing that is the difference between a novice and an old-timer.

Getting Your Bearings Off-Trail

How do you prevent getting lost off the trail? Plan well, stay highly alert and observant, and keep track of both what's ahead and behind you. First, pre-plot your route carefully. Know, for example, that it will take you over a ridge, along the flank of a 10,000-foot peak, down a granite field, then up a stream and through a meadow toward the lake. Keep these features on the surface of your mind. Before you leave the trail, take a hard look around for all distinctive landmarks: a strange rock outcropping, a tall barren tree once struck by lightning and thus black against the green forest, a distant mountain peak. Note what lies in the direction you're headed. Think how the appearance of these landmarks will change as you hike cross-country. And look for what features you know are on your route.

You may or may not plan to return by the same route. Nevertheless, you may *need* to get back to the trail at this same spot, especially if your route proves impassable and you must turn around. Thus, you might want to mark your trail. Cairns, colored ribbons strung on branches and retrieved if you return, green vegetation hung on a barren branch — all give you a sense of confidence that is more than worth the additional time you spend doing it. Also, if you do intend to come back the way you went in, a marked course will save you one final embarrassment — walking right past the maintained trail. It's surprisingly easy to miss an "obvious" trail, and frustrating, doubling back till you do find it. If you mark everything from the start, you can avoid that problem on a day when you may have to hike out, drive home, and go to work.

More precise than sighted landmarks or marked routes is a combined use of the topo map and a compass. They can help you decide where you are and where your destination is relative to you. There are whole books on the use of compass and maps (see "Appendix"); what we give you here is a quick digest of the main points. Whether you have a compass or not, practice with the topo map on the trail, before you really need it. When you reach open places, try to locate yourself on the map by observation alone. Do this by orienting the map to 2 or more observable landmarks, then draw imaginary (or real) lines from them back toward "yourself." Where the lines intersect is approximately where you are. (See ILLUSTRATION A.)

Now do the same thing with your compass. First orient the map. That means getting it aligned with the real world out there. Set the map

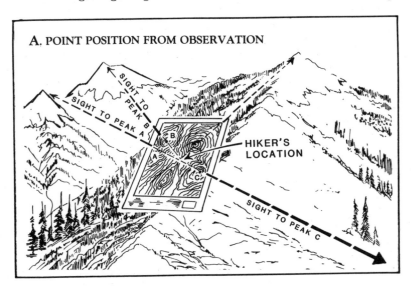

A. POINT POSITION FROM OBSERVATION

SIGHT TO PEAK B

SIGHT TO PEAK A

HIKER'S LOCATION

SIGHT TO PEAK C

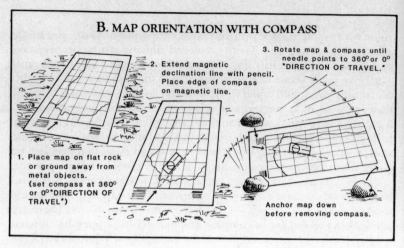

B. MAP ORIENTATION WITH COMPASS

2. Extend magnetic declination line with pencil. Place edge of compass on magnetic line.

3. Rotate map & compass until needle points to 360° or 0° "DIRECTION OF TRAVEL."

1. Place map on flat rock or ground away from metal objects. (set compass at 360° or 0° "DIRECTION OF TRAVEL")

Anchor map down before removing compass.

on a flat rock, placing the edge of your compass on the magnetic north (MN) declination line marked on the bottom margin of the map, and twist map and compass together until the north-pointing needle is lined up with the 36O or O degrees mark on the compass. (See ILLUSTRATION B.) Now your map is properly aligned and you're ready to go to work. Take sightings on 2 or more identifiable landmarks, the farther away (though still represented on your map) the better. Here's how you take a sighting. Hold the compass in your hand. Point the Direction-of-Travel arrow toward the landmark. (The assumption here is that you have an "orienteering" compass. See ILLUSTRATION C.) Now twist the compass housing till the north-pointing needle is lined up with the orienting arrow at the bottom of the housing. That's all. Just read the number of degrees which come up on the edge of the housing facing the landmark.

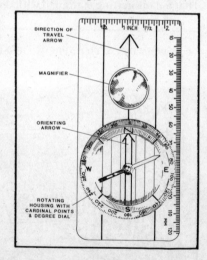

DIRECTION OF TRAVEL ARROW

MAGNIFIER

ORIENTING ARROW

ROTATING HOUSING WITH CARDINAL POINTS & DEGREE DIAL

If you don't have an orienteering compass, do this: Face the landmark, holding the compass in front of you. Slowly rotate the compass till its north-pointing needle lines up with the N on the housing. Don't rotate yourself! New read the number of degrees facing the landmark.

Say the reading is 330 degrees, as in ILLUSTRATION D.Once you have a 1st reading, take a 2nd or 3rd on other landmarks,the farther from each other the better. In ILLUSTRATION D, the second reading is 32 degrees. Now go back to your oriented map, set one edge of the compass on the first landmark and then rotate the compass, still keeping the edge in contact with the landmark, till the north-pointing needle again lines up with the orienting arrow, giving you a 330 degrees reading on the map.Draw a line along the compass edge back toward yourself. Repeat for the second landmark and maybe a third. Where the lines intersect is where you are. You can now determine from the map how much farther it is and how rough the terrain will be between your present location and your destination.

A final word of caution. Your sightings, readings and orientings may be correct but there is still a chance you'll end up with approximate, rather than pinpoint locations. You may trudge on for an hour, reach the top of a rise and expect to see the promised lake. Instead you see another rise, like the bear that went over the mountain. You take more readings and bearings and come up with the same results. You have moved, but those distant peaks on which you sighted are so far and so high that to them you haven't moved at all. Keep the faith, check your progress *vis-a-vis* closer landmarks, and take it slow and easy. The lake is there, over one or 2 more rises, and if the footing is sure and the sun is up, you'll arrive in time to unpack, set up camp, drop a line and cook a fine trout supper.

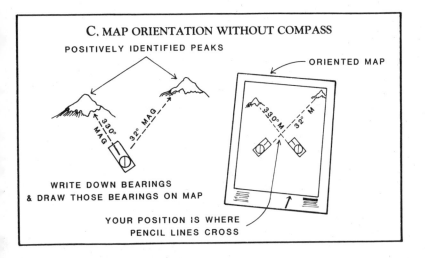

C. MAP ORIENTATION WITHOUT COMPASS

POSITIVELY IDENTIFIED PEAKS

ORIENTED MAP

330° MAG

32° MAG

330° M

32° M

WRITE DOWN BEARINGS
& DRAW THOSE BEARINGS ON MAP

YOUR POSITION IS WHERE
PENCIL LINES CROSS

PART THREE:
Being
There

CHAPTER V:
Setting Up Camp

Choosing A Lake

Most really spectacular lakes have well-maintained trails to them. A trail usually means the lake is accessible both to people on foot and to groups on horseback. The crowds at these lakes can be oppressive, especially on weekends and holidays. We like to get off privately, to swim, sun and have fun. Usually this means scouring the map for a mountain lake without a trail to it, one we can call our own if only for a few days.

We also love to catch, cook and eat trout — another consideration when seeking an off-trail lake on the map. Trout require a lake deep enough that it won't freeze solid during the winter. Lakes at or near the treeline get colder sooner and remain frozen longer, and cannot support the insectlife that fish need to survive. And there's very little nearby firewood. For a 3 or 4 day stretch, choose a lower elevation lake with water flowing through it, though don't plan on catching anything but mosquitos at a lake surrounded by meadows; you might find nothing but mud when you get there. Steep cliffs and sheer rock walls rising from one bank are an indication of a deep section, which may contain fish.

Choosing A Campsite

Plan to make your camp at either the inlet or outlet of the lake, where you'll possibly find an old campsite complete with fireplace, cleared tent area, and a path to the stream, an unbeatable convenience when you want to fetch a pail of water. Because water is the first essential of a multi-day campsite. A clear, fast-flowing stream gives the best, which, unless you're warned otherwise when you get a wilderness permit, is safe to drink and cook with. In fact, it tastes a lot better than almost any water you'll ever drink out of a pipe. Many backpackers enjoy mountain water so much they have no need of Kool-Aid, lemonade, or any other powdered pick-me-ups. The purity and safety of lake water is a little more questionable. Early in the spring, as snows are melting and lakes are full, lake water is clear and clean. Late in the fall it may get a layer of dirt and scum at the top near shore, and you might wish to wade out for your drinking water.

We don't personally know anyone who has ever become ill from mountain water. But as more people take to the backcountry, the water invariably becomes more polluted. We've been warned about drinking untreated water in certain areas of both California and Hawaii. These warnings concern intestinal bugs (bacteria, parasites and amoebas) that are transmitted by waste products of both humans and animals. Even if all the people are downstream, animal wastes could pollute the water at your campsite, so it must often be treated. Avoiding certain diseases, such as giardia, requires boiling the water; others can be prevented by treating the water with purification tablets. Boiling takes lots of time, energy and fuel; treating the water with tablets is simpler. Just drop a tablet into a canteenful and wait 10 or 15 minutes. The water tastes like it came out of a swimming pool.

At times you won't have access to running water. Streams may be dried up. You may want or have to spend a night on a ridge or peak. There is nothing as spectacular as the night sky seen from a summit; in fact, the sunsets and sunrises alone make it well worth the inconvenience of carrying water up there. We figure about a quart per person will get us through dinner and a morning hike down without doing any dishes. We wash them later when we get to the next stream or lake (though never *in* the stream or lake).

Many backpackers bring a collapsible, 2-gallon container for storing water at the campsite. This is especially convenient if the camp is some distance from the water — for example, when your desired site at the best water source is already occupied, and you need to move a long way from lake or stream. In the absence of such a container, make do by filling all your pots and canteens, then covering them with lids or metal plates. Do this before dark: it's hard to carry 2 pots of water and hold a flashlight as you scamper up a steep grade to your campsite.

Tentsite

The sole requirement for a tentsite is that you can sleep there. This means different things to different people. We knew one old-timer who never carried an ensolite pad. Instead, he'd stop early in the afternoon and work for at least 2 hours preparing his sleeping site. He meticulously smoothed the earth, picked out all the rocks and twigs, then laid down a soft bed of pine needles and fallen leaves. Finally he spread his sleeping bag down on the soft bed just in time to go fishing.

Before you choose a tentsite, look carefully at the drainage system of the surrounding hills. More than once we've set up in a likely-looking area, flat and sandy, near a lake, only to discover it turned into a large mud puddle in the rain. Mountain rains often come suddenly and hard. Flat sandy areas can become Lake Superior in 20 or 30 minutes, putting you and your tent 2 or 3 inches under water.

Some people dig a little ditch around their tentsite to route rain water away from the tent floor and thus stay dry from the bottom up. It's a very uncomfortable feeling to be securely under your waterproof rainfly and notice a puddle in one corner inching across the tent toward you. And if it's really pouring, there's not much you can do then except slosh around until the storm passes, make do as well as you can that night, and hope for warm sunshine in the morning to dry yourself out. Be aware, however, that if those ditches are over-elaborate, they will harm the natural environment by creating erosion networks.

Another consideration in choosing a tentsite is the ability to stake your tent. While newer dome-type tents do not require stakes, most small tents need secure staking in the ground. This makes them difficult to set up in granite or sandy areas. In such spots, lay the stake flat on the ground and pile rocks on top of it, or wedge it in a granite rift.

Sometimes you can tie the tent ropes to boulders or tree branches instead of to stakes. Sandy campsites present similar problems: the stakes shift easily or pull out. Every time the tent is bumped, the stakes slip a little and pretty soon the tent sags like a suspension bridge. Both rocky and sandy areas require extra care when you enter or leave the tent.

You'll probably rarely have to clear your own tentsite. Wherever the trail meets a source of water, you'll usually find a campsite cleared and ready (and possibly occupied!). The campsite invariably consists of at least one tentsite and fireplace. Usually there are several of each.

Many people backpack with only a sleeping bag and poncho. The poncho can be rigged up between or under trees or bushes to form a roof and keep you out of the rain. As long as the ground stays fairly dry, such shelter is adequate for most summer showers. A tentless pack is that much lighter, but it takes a fair amount of ingenuity to stay dry in stormy weather (to say nothing of mosquito-proofing). And a wet sleeping bag can take days to dry out. Even if you plan to sleep under the stars, put up your tent as a precaution. Nothing changes faster in the mountains than the weather.

Campfires

Campfires have a magic all their own. Staring into the fire late at night gives you a sense of peace and security that is hard to match at home. Our trips into the mountains center around hot meals, which invariably center around the campfire. Cooking, baking, sipping hot chocolate, heating water for dishes or washing up, all require a well-tended hearth.

Wilderness campfires consume tremendous quantities of wood, however. In many areas of the mountains that wood is becoming very scarce, and fires are not permitted. This is particularly true at high elevations and along well-traveled trails. Even where it's legal to gather wood for a campfire, it's often obvious that there is little dead wood left and that the environment can't take any more tampering with. Consider the ecology of the camping area before building a campfire. And when necessary, sacrifice the fire to preserve the beauty of the site. Use the stove instead and cook your meals quickly.

Let's assume though, that you're camped at a lower elevation lake or stream, a couple of miles off the trail. There's plenty of dry wood on the ground. You plan to stay here a couple days and your mouth is already watering with culinary intentions. First you need a fireplace.

A backcountry fireplace is nothing more than a circle of rocks with

dirt in the middle. Fires feed a constant shower of sparks into the air. When there's little wind, these are entirely harmless. But a sudden gust can blow the sparks toward combustible material, and you can quickly have a forest fire on your hands. If your campsite already has a fireplace, use it. Just be sure to clear the ground for 4 or 5 feet in all directions and check for dead, dry branches hanging less than 10 feet directly over the fire area.

For cooking and baking, we usually modify existing fireplaces, or construct from scratch new ones of our own design. The back of the fireplace is made narrow to support a small camp grill. The front of the fireplace has one or 2 rocks that are easy to remove. We clear an additional area in front of these for baking, and surround this area with a ring of stones. At baking time, we remove both rocks, and rake hot coals into this ring. Meanwhile, we can heat dishwater or stir-fry vegetables on the back grill.

As you construct different campsites, you'll get different ideas on how to modify the basic fireplace to meet your needs. If a wobbly rock sends a full pot of water tumbling into the fire, you won't let that happen the next night: you'll firm up the rocks, creating a stable base for the impending souffle. Next you may discover there isn't enough draft the way this fireplace is constructed, and you'll need to build the back higher than the sides. And you'll doubtless find that the artistic fireplace you come across at the Arcadian lake of your dreams is just too big for your one pot. It would be fine for U.S. Steel or a party of 30 with mules, but... So you hack and haul, sculpting a new, smaller, lighter and more efficient version on the same site.

It's useful to collect firewood in a variety of sizes. Small dry twigs are great for starting fires, but burn too quickly for cooking. Large, long logs burn for hours, but won't fit under the grill for heating a pot of water. We bring a camp saw to cut large logs into shorter, easy-to-use lengths, which last longer. The saw is lightweight, folds into itself for safety, and can be sharpened at a saw shop between trips. It is *never ever* used on living trees, only on uprooted deadfall wood.

If you have to go far to gather the wood, bring a poncho to carry smaller pieces back to camp in fewer trips. But don't use it as a sack; it's guaranteed to tear. Rather, wrap the wood in the poncho and cradle the whole load in your arms. We also take a pair of garden gloves which help save the hands when we gather firewood. They also double as pot-holder mittens. In the cooking chapter, we tell you how to use the fire most efficiently.

Starting A Fire

Late in the summer, in a forested campsite, you'll find plenty of dry kindling. If you can bend a twig back against itself without breaking it, it's too wet for kindling. The best kindling will snap in 2 with a loud crack as soon as you bend it.

Start with the smallest, driest kindling you have. Keep a pile of it in reserve to add to the first flames. Remember that fires need lots of air. Too much fuel creates too much smoke which keeps the air away, so the fire goes out. Start your fire with a small, well-ventilated flame at the bottom, a space for air, then another layer of wood. You can shape this like a teepee, a lean-to, or a log cabin. Make sure the kindling is burning well before adding larger pieces of wood.

So far so good. It's easy to start a fire with good dry kindling. But what if it's wet? Old-timers may tell you to break lower branches off live trees for kindling. These lowest limbs are actually deadwood and, if they fan out into small twigs, are fine for starting a fire even in rain or

snow. But the idea of breaking dead branches from living trees is ecologically repugnant. Most campsites are surrounded by stripped trees for a 100 yards in all directions. It looks like the area was bombed from the bottom up. Don't break branches off trees *except in an emergency*.

We often use the pages of our paperbacks to start fires. We usually read 30-70 pages a day, between trailside rest stops and afternoon cooking sessions, so we have plenty to burn. Paper or cardboard from food containers is also great for starting fires.

Another easy way to start fires is to use a flammable liquid or gel. If you have a kerosene or alcohol stove, the fuel can start wood burning in wet conditions. Some people bring a small can of lighter fluid for emergency fire starting. If you do use a flammable liquid, *never* pour any onto a fire that is already lit or smoldering. It may ignite the can you're pouring from! You can also buy fire starter in a tube, like toothpaste.

Okay. The kindling is burning, whether it's dry or wet. Now for the larger pieces. The point is to build a fire gradually. Onto the kindling go larger dry branches. When they're well lit and flaming (not smoking), place a log or 2 gently on top, leaving plenty of air space between the pieces of fuel. Larger logs are likely to be dry inside. Once you get them burning, they'll keep burning even in a drizzle or mist. If there's protection above them, they'll burn in the rain. We often place a layer of rain-dampened logs about 3 feet above the fire between two piles of rocks. This wooden roof protects the fire from rain and dries the logs at the same time. When these logs get dry enough to burn, they can be pushed into the fire and replaced. With a little ingenuity, you can cook and eat in the rain without much trouble.

One last word on fire-starting frustrations. The fire has started. The cardboard is burning. You add some more wood, but it's wet and the fire starts to go out. Frantically, you squeeze some fire starter onto a stick and throw it into the embers. It flares up, flames for a minute, then dies again. What now? Our advice is to stop, let it go out and start over from the beginning. We've seen novices waste reams of paper and tubes of fire starter trying to burn wet wood.

Remember, a good fire starts with good kindling. The second time, gather drier twigs and branches, even if you have to walk deeper into the forest to find them. Keep a larger supply of dry twigs to add to the fire as it starts to burn. It will work: guaranteed! And at the next campsite, you'll gather the right combination of wood sizes and dryness to start the fire easily the first time.

Food Storage

Little Critters

The squirrel family is undeniably cute. All of them: chipmunks, prairie dogs, ground squirrels. They are positively Disney Worldish in their lovability. They'll approach fairly close, stand up on hind legs, rub front paws together and chirp. It's tempting to reward them with a morsel or two. Squirrels are also smart and voracious; they're world-class experts at stealing your stash. Chewing through a pack and several layers of plastic and cardboard is child's play for them, leaving you with a shortfall of precious food.

A cardinal rule of backpacking is *never feed the animals*. It is unfair *and* dangerous. Instead of applying themselves to their natural food, they've discovered an easier, tastier way to fill up. If you feed them or leave leftover food behind, it makes them dependent and renders them less able to survive in their natural habitat. That's the danger to them. The danger to you, aside from the loss of some closely-budgeted food, is a possible bite, which can be painful and sometimes septic.

A family or two of rodents living around any well-used campground is inevitable. They come out mostly at night and look for food. They are so used to finding food in backpacks that they will often chew through your pack even when all food has been removed and hung high in a stuffsack. All edibles should be hung up at night, if possible, (see illustration, p. 98). Should you find rodent toothmarks on your cheese, just cut off the chewed portion and eat the rest. We've never heard of anyone getting sick by eating the untouched part. And a nibble-sized hole in a pack or pouch is easily sewn up.

We react similarly to ants and bees, brushing off those in the packets and eating the food. These insects can be kept out by packing food in tightly sealed plastic bags. Another common problem is food spilled inside the pack. The pack was set flat on the ground instead of upright, and the maple syrup, like flowing water, sought and found its natural level. Clean up as you might, the ants and bees will love that pack even when it's empty. But they never seem to do any harm.

The Long Hot Summer

Our worst problem with food is storage on hot days. Keeping your stash out of the mid-summer sun in a rocky campsite can be a 14-hour struggle. Not all food is harmed by excessive heat, but cheese, eggs, chocolate among others, are. At the beginning of the trip you tend to throw chocolate bars into nooks and crannies of the pack to save space. But if they're not double-bagged in plastic, and if you set your pack down in the blazing, afternoon sun, you'll have a melted chocolate mess oozing throughout your pack. If there are no deep shade trees around camp, figure out other ways of keeping food out of the sun. Sometimes the shady side of an old tree trunk works; a rock ledge may have a shady spot at its base; you might rig a poncho or tarp to block the sun from the food pack. Don't leave food in the tent all day: tent fabric is so thin it works more like a greenhouse than a refrigerator.

Bears

We've heard lots of bear stories: automobile trunks ripped open by powerful paws; mama-and-cub teams getting to "bear-proof" bags hanging high on guy wires strung between trees; meeting bears on trails; and even "playing dead," hoping that a bear wouldn't maul a camper after it ate all his food several feet away. We even have a few stories of our own, but like taxi stories, enough is enough. The point is that if you take a few precautions, you can share the wilderness safely even with the big critters.

The most important rule for dealing with bears is to be forewarned. Find out about them and plan a strategy before you reach bear country. Ask the ranger when you apply for your permit. Consult with the guard at the park entrance. Try to plan your trip to avoid campsites that have a reputation for bear troubles.

Bear-Proofing The Food Stash

If you're going to problem areas, learn if there are bear-proof wires at certain campsites. These are steel cables, about 3/8 inch thick, strung about 20 feet off the ground between 2 stout tree trunks. If there are wires, you only need 50 feet of rope and 2 stuffsacks. Here's what you do:

Divide your food between the stuffsacks. Throw one end of the rope over the wire (tying a rock to it will help). Tie a stuffsack to the other

end. Hoist the stuffsack about 20 feet into the air. Tie your other stuffsack to the rope as high as you can reach. The 2 sacks should roughly
balance each other, one about 6 feet off the ground, the other about 20
feet up. Don't leave any extra rope hanging; stuff it inside the sack.
With a long stick, raise the bottom sack as high as you can. Raising it to
about 15 feet will lower the other sack to about the same height. There
you have it: 2 food-laden stuffsacks suspended about 15 feet off the
ground. The wire is too thick for a bear to cut or tear and the sacks are

too high for mom or her cubs to reach. You can sleep soundly. In the morning you'll need a pole long enough to push one sack up until the other is low enough to grab. Usually such a pole sits next to the wire and is easy to recognize.

If rangers or other campers tell you of a bear problem and there are no bear-proof wires in the area, you have several options. The first is to camp elsewhere. Bears don't *naturally* bother people or eat their food. They learn over time, like squirrels, that it's easier than foraging. They tend to have a territory that they regularly patrol in search of campers, foodsacks and garbage; if you're on their route, they'll try their luck with your goods. The farther away you get, the less likely they'll come to your campsite. An extra afternoon of hiking will often give you enough room that you needn't worry. Hiking 3 miles from that scenic lake and camping along a stream might save a week's food.

A second option is to rig up your own bear-proof system of hanging food sacks. Getting a tight line 20 feet off the ground between 2 trees isn't easy, but it is possible if you persevere. Or you might just hoist the food 15 feet up by looping it over a single high branch. Another plan is to use a cliff ledge. While bears can climb trees, they cannot climb rock faces. If you find a cliff or ledge 12-15 feet up, and if you can reach it, the bear won't be able to.

The third choice is just to leave the food in your pack or in a stuff-sack on the ground. You might fasten some cups or forks or spoons onto the drawstrings. Then go to sleep and hope that 1) no bear appears, 2) failing that, you hear it beginning to rustle your food, and 3) you are in the presence of one timid enough to be scared away by a furless, claw-less and fangless human being banging pots and throwing rocks. We've done it and it's worked. But be careful. It's better to lose your food or your pack than to wrestle an angry bear.

Grizzlies

Outside Glacier and Yellowstone national parks and Alaska, most of the bears you'll encounter in the wilderness are black bears. They're interested in your food, but aren't intent on doing you any harm. What if you meet such a bear on the trail? If you remain calm and back off, the bear will probably do the same. Don't get between a mama and her cub; don't surprise or scare a bear; and never back one into a corner. If you're worried about bumping into bears on the trail, make a lot of noise as you hike. Forewarned, the bear will avoid you.

Grizzly bears (and their relatives, brown bears) are something else. The only major grizzly populations in the Lower 48 are in Glacier and

Yellowstone. Here the bears are very dangerous, being garbage-fed and unpredictable. They have been known to hurt people, seemingly for no reason. When antagonized, it's possible they'll attack instead of waddling off. If you're entering grizzly country, you have to be much more careful. One veteran put together these rules:

- Always make a lot of noise as you walk.
- Try to hike with others. Numbers sometimes discourage bears.
- Leave the dogs at home. They can rouse a grizzly to a fright and fury.
- Camp, when possible, near a climbable tree. (Grizzlies don't climb trees.)
- Try to cook (and hang your food at night) 200-300 yards downwind of your sleeping area. Have a separate set of "cooking clothes" and hang them up also with your food at night.
- Never bang a pot or throw a rock at a grizzly.
- Carry a spare stuff sack. If the grizzly gets your food, you'll still have a sack for your sleeping bag.

Stormy Weather

Most first-time backpackers have a negative attitude about rain, considering it "bad" weather. At home, you don't go out into the rain or cold for fun. You stay indoors, turn the thermostat up, and watch TV. The backpacking equivalent of that attitude is to set up the tent, put on the rainfly, and curl up in your sleeping bag until the sun comes out. It doesn't take long to realize the quarters are a lot more cramped in a puptent than in your living room. You get claustrophobic; you want to stretch; every time you go out for a snack, you track water back into the tent; soon, you start to get depressed about the weather.

There is a different attitude toward stormy weather, however, one worth cultivating. The rain is another mood of the mountains, creating a unique beauty in altered sounds, smells and perspectives. Get out of your tent and enjoy it. In fact, we often take our tent down when it starts to rain and use the ground cloth and rainfly to make a porch and covered cooking area. We store the packs under plastic garbage bags. Once the clothes and sleeping bags are secure, we can go about our business. We read in the rain, cook in the rain, fish in the rain (often the best fishing), and sometimes just sit and watch the lightning in the distance, listen to the thunder as it rolls closer, and view the rain-washed lake and mountains.

Then the storm passes and the skies begin to clear. As long as you stay warm with several layers of clothes, and dry with a poncho on you or strung up above you, you can weather bad weather in good spirits.

There is no such thing as "normal" mountain weather. The hottest days often come in September. July thundershowers can turn to hail and snow at upper elevations. A clear morning can be followed by a wet, miserable afternoon. You have to be prepared for it all. Our guidelines are:

- A poncho for every person.
- A rainfly and groundcloth for every tent.
- A garbage bag for every pack.

These are conservative. Many people do it with less. The more you've done it, the better you can manage with less protection. It's frustrating to pack rain gear around for 9 or 10 days and never use it. On the other hand, people who pack in less rain gear often plan to do more hiking each day. Since it's more likely to rain in the afternoon in the mountains, they plan to hike in it and need only keep themselves and their packs dry. Our idea of backpacking stations us at a campsite most afternoons, either because we hike only in the morning or because we stay in one place for 2 or 3 days at a time. So when we see that first hailstone bounce off the ground, the extra gear is suddenly worth its weight in gold.

Washing Up

Pollution in the high country is disheartening and unnecessary. If you find a gum wrapper on the trail, you can pick it up and carry it out yourself. But if you see soapsuds along the shore of a lake, it's too late to do anything about it. Don't let detergent get into the water in the first place—that's the only time to stop it.

Never wash dishes in a lake or stream. Carry them and a pot of hot water at least 100 feet away into the forest. Put 2 drops of biodegradable liquid soap in a small pot, then add about a third of the hot water. Wash each dish or pot with this until the food particles are gone. Rinse out the sponge, then rinse each dish with the clean sponge and the remaining hot water. One pot is plenty for all the washing up after a 4-person meal. If even that amount of soap offends you, do without it. A good scrubbing with a "toughy" or even pine needles gets utensils clean. Using the same washing spot for several days will attract flies and bees. If it's 20 or 30 yards from camp, you'll be spared the buzzing and bother.

Do your laundry the same way. One soapy pot and one rinse pot are enough for 2 people to wash shirts, socks and underwear. Often, a good rinse without soap will get socks or shirt ready for a morning hike. Even then, the dirty water shouldn't go into the lake or stream; dump it onto the ground.

Cleaning yourself should also be done away from the stream or lake. Heat a pot to a comfortable temperature. Find a scenic spot back in the forest, away from the lake. Then soap and rinse. You can even do a fine job of washing your hair. Just have someone help you with the rinse.

Don't soap up and jump into the lake or stream to rinse off. Even if the label says "biodegradable," the suds will be around killing fish and insects until next spring. Rinse yourself thoroughly so the soap soaks into the ground. When you go for a swim, leave the water as unpolluted as you found it.

Finally, there's the matter of a toilet. Rule of thumb is 100 *yards* from any water; the farther the better. Dig a hole at least 4 or 5 inches deep. Cover thoroughly when you're finished. Pack it down. Don't bury toilet paper. While organic waste will decompose quickly, toilet paper may take years. Bring it back to camp and throw it into the fire or put it in the garbage bag to burn later. The same rules apply to tampons and sanitary napkins: burn, don't bury.

Planning A Day Trip

Securing camp before you set off to climb a mountain or fish at a nearby lake is simple. Prepare for hot sun, heavy rain or a ripping wind; any or all could happen while you're gone. Keep food in the shade, leave a rainfly over the tent, and batten down the hatches just in case.

The more difficult question is, what do you take with you? We carry a poncho for rain, a down parka for cold, a map and compass for guidance, sunglasses for glare, a flashlight in case we misjudge the time, water and a big lunch. If you plan several day trips, you might consider investing in a sleeping bag stuffsack which can be fitted with a shoulder strap from your backpack. Ask about this at a camping store. You won't have the extra weight of a daypack, but can carry everything on your back during your explorations of the nearby country.

We once climbed a Sierra peak and found a 2-page typed story in the sign-in book that had been placed there several years earlier. It concerned 3 young backpackers who left their camp late one afternoon in shirt sleeves and shorts to climb a nearby peak. They made it up with ease and saw a climbable ridge to the next peak. It was a challenge and they took it. The sun was close to the horizon when they got to the top of the second peak, but the ridge kept going up to the highest peak in the range. They were really pumping and couldn't turn back. On they went.

They reached the top of the highest peak just as the sun set. Sure enough, it was a gorgeous view and a magnificent sunset. But what should they do now? They had no warm clothes and couldn't spend the night. They had no food, no water. They had no map, no flashlight. The way they had come up was too treacherous to go down in the dark. As they talked, it grew darker and colder. They couldn't stay, they had to keep moving.

One of the party remembered an alternate route down. The others would try anything to keep active and stay warm. They followed him in the dark. The story told of scraped knees and elbows, scrambling, rockslides. Dawn found them still together at the base of a steep cliff fighting their way through the brush to get to a river. Then they had to work their way up river without a trail until they finally stumbled into their camp, a full 24-four hours after they'd set out. They were lucky no one was hurt. They were lucky to be alive. The following summer, one of them typed their story and left it atop the mountain. That time, he climbed up with map, food, and warm clothes. Just in case.

Daytrip Destinations

Where can you go for the day? Easiest is a hike along a trail to a ridge, pass, peak or lake that you would miss via your planned route. Hiking with a light daypack is a real joy after several days of struggling with all that weight on your shoulders. You'll cover a lot more ground, and whether you bring a good book, a camera or a picnic lunch, it's a fine way to pass some daylight hours.

Fishing buffs will often spend the day exploring a stream or fishing at a nearby lake. Stream fishing can be very successful on a daytrip. You can try pools and white-water areas that may never have been fished before because they are far from the normal trails. Lake fishing is less likely to be successful, because you invariably end up fishing at the worst time of the day. It's nearly noon when you get there, and you have to leave around 2 or 3 o'clock to return to camp by sundown. As long as you don't mind a slow few hours of fishing, it can be a scenic and relaxing day.

Mountain climbers will want to spend a day climbing a nearby peak. Plan the route in advance using the topo map. Make sure you can come back down the same way you climbed up. Often you'll get to a ridge near the top and find a sheer 30-foot wall. For some, that's the point to stop, take some pictures, and turn around. Others, with more courage, experience or equipment, might continue.

Two words of caution. First, don't plan to go down via a new route. If you encounter that 30-foot drop from above, you're in trouble. Second, if the way is not clear, mark it as you go so you'll be able to return safely and with ease.

Another idea: check out a cross-country route which looks promising on the map but which you aren't sure is possible with a full pack. A daytrip with the minimum weight is just the ticket. You can backtrack, scout the best line, double check steep or dangerous spots, mark the trail, and return to camp ready to set out the next day with a full pack and the promise of yet another hidden lake found and fished.

Hanging Out

Let's face it. A lot of people won't want to shlep off to climb another peak or hike another mile after they've worked hard to reach that picture-perfect campsite. They want to stay put. The fine art of hanging out was developed by just such people. And an art it is! Not everyone is satisfied sitting still or puttering with small projects or incidental pleasures. We've learned, for instance, that the younger the person, the greater the chance of getting bored just hanging around camp. We've also met solo backpackers who need to contrive detailed daily schedules while in camp to keep the lonely-blues away.

Basically, hanging out depends on what you like to do. Karen fishes for approximately 27 hours a day and is reluctant to permit the sun to set. She is sublimely happy to hear an 800-page novel read aloud while she casts. Eva and Stanya, our meat-and-potatoes crew, have been known to spend an hour or so rearranging the food stash so the cookies and chocolate can be got at 3 micro-seconds faster when a munchy emergency strikes. Drew, the Lost Dutchman, loves above all things to triangulate our position with one of those super Swedish orienteering compasses. He patiently sits for hours finding us as if we were lost. He has never quite got the hang of it, but he seems not to care. In fact, success might cut down or eliminate altogether his pleasure in the trying.

We're not anxious to reveal how many mystery novels have started evening fires after they've been consumed by ravenous who-dunnit buffs. Virgil, our old-time friend who only backpacks alone, writes poems and space fantasies for endless contented hours deep in the mountains. We've known people to begin watching and enjoying the sunset at noon. We didn't ask questions. Tent, pack, and pants mending often go beyond necessity to sheer pleasure. Peter, the original junk food junkie and also a lead guitarist in a local rock 'n roll band, spent much of his first backpacking trip composing long, soulful tunes to Mars Bars and Reese's Peanut Butter Cups. He missed them. Inventions and discoveries happen while hanging out. Junk food Peter and his friend Carol found themselves down to their last beloved crossword puzzle 16 miles deep into the Sierra backcountry. They grieved for a few minutes and then, inspired by notions of self-help, got to work with Rick to produce the first all-weather backpacker's crossword. Rick and Hal began this book hanging out one day years ago; if you turn to Chapter VII and read the tale of the fabled Hidden Lake Souffle, you'll see the first words we put down on paper. Active or passive, intro- or extrovert, gregarious or a loner, the possibilities for finding pleasure in hanging out are endless. You've come a long way. Now's the time to enjoy.

CHAPTER VI: Fishing

The sky is cloudless, a deep indigo. The sun has already set. It's surprising how fast the warmth vanishes when the sun goes down. A cool breeze blows from the west. Time for parka and knit cap.

We've been fishing from the lakeshore for about an hour without a bite. Almost in a trance, Rick casts a lure into the depths of the lake and reels it back slowly: twitching it, stopping, speeding up; casting left, then right; trying to run it deep, then shallow. Hal goes on reading *Catch 22* aloud. Milo Minderbinder has cornered the world market on guns and is moving in on butter.

A slight tug on Rick's line brings his thoughts back to the lake. Is it a fish nibbling at the lure or just a snag on some undergrowth? To find out he slows down the lure, twitches it a little, keeps it moving very slowly. Another tug, and Rick says, "Hey, I think I've got one!"

Half a ton of live, angry fish breaks the surface to our left. The body completely leaves the water, a full 6 inches above the ripples, then splashes back under the surface. That's when Rick notices his line peeling off the reel. The monster fish is the one on his line.

Rick tightens up on the drag. Not too much, though; that fellow could easily snap his light line. His heart pounds; his hands tremble. This is one big fish.

Reel it in; let it run out on the drag. Reel it in; let it go out again. The fish is getting tired. Rick's getting tired too. The line gets shorter as man coaxes fish toward the shore. Now we can see it: weary, slightly canted to the side. It's in about 3 feet of water below the rock we stand on. But it's too heavy to yank out, and we have no net.

Like walking a dog, Rick slowly leads the fish along the rocky bank to a muddy inlet about 15 feet away. Every 3 or 4 feet, the fish twitches. But it's exhausted and hurt. Rick drags it closer to the muddy incline. Now it is in only 4 inches of water. Then, with a steady pull, he lands the fish. It flops a few times on the beach, but the line holds. Rick reaches down, unhooks it, and puts it in a pot: a 16-inch Golden trout.

Rick starts to speak, but nothing comes out. His heart is pounding; he feels a little dizzy. Ten minutes of play has felt like an hour's work. He sits down. Leaning against a rock, eyes closed, it takes ten minutes more to get back to normal. And then in only an hour, Rick and Hal sit down to the finest, freshest trout amandine dinner they've ever eaten.

Someone once described a firefighter's job as hours and hours of utter boredom punctuated by a few moments of sheer terror. We could describe mountain fishing as hours and hours of pure relaxation punctuated by a few moments of wild excitement. The most enjoyable part of high mountain fishing is the relaxation: the scenery, the weather, the routine of casting, retrieving and playing the lure or fly.

The picture hanging above Rick's desk at work is not of a string of 14-inch trout. Rather, it's a shot of him casting into a mountain lake at sunset. The peaks above are nearly orange; you can see their reflection in the lake. Standing on a spit of land, his figure is a silhouette against the pale sky. More than anything else, we recommend high country fishing for the beauty and quiet pleasure it brings. The tasty trout are but an additional bonus.

Mountain Trout: A Fish's Eye View

Winter

If you've never fished for trout before, a good place to begin learning is to experience the lake as the fish does – in the mind's eye of a high-mountain lake trout. During the winter the lake surface is covered with snow and ice. The water below is close to freezing, and only a little nourishment flows through. The trout, being cold-blooded, respond appropriately: as the temperature descends, so does their metabolism. Though they continue feeding all winter, they need very little food. If you could get into high country in the dead of winter, you'd work very hard to get through the ice for a fish.

In early spring, which in the mountains means late May and early June, the fishing is also often lean. Occasionally we've camped at a high lake just as spring is breaking. Parts of the lake are still frozen. And just 5 or 10 feet from shore, huge trout swim slowly along, evidently there for the taking. But nothing seems to work: flies, lures, moving bait are universally ignored. Sometimes the fish feed on a small worm or grub buried in the mud. But basically they're just out sunning, warming themselves in the water's upper layers. There's not much to eat yet and the fish aren't hungry. Neither the spawning cycle (which produces lots of yummy eggs) nor the insect hatching cycle (which produces a living feast) have yet begun. As Br'er Rabbit would observe, "They're layin' low."

Spring: June And Early July

The longer, warmer days of June and early July melt the snow rapidly. Suddenly, water is everywhere. Lakes are overflowing. Meadows turn emerald with lush growth and are dappled with wild flowers. The insect hatch begins. From tiny eggs, insect larvae appear, little white worms called grubs or nymphs which live in the shallows of lakes or streams.

As the lake begins warming, and the fishes' body temperatures rise, the trout start moving faster. They quickly get hungry. And as the snow melts in the mountain meadows, it washes small grubs down through the lake, so the fish don't have to look far for food. They congregate at the places in the lake where they can find shelter, comfort, and food.

Where are these spots? Shelter could mean deep water. However, trout aren't too comfortable in the deepest part of the lake: there's little food, less oxygen, and the cold temperatures make them sluggish. In the spring, as the ice melts, the upper 40 feet of the lake will have a good supply of oxygen and water of the right temperature. Shelter in this region might be available under a bank or beneath a rock overhang.

To trout, the food question is simple: how to get the most food for the least energy? In the springtime, they do this by finding a quiet place next to a food-bearing flow of water. This allows them to watch the current passively, then dart into it only to ingest food. In mountain lakes, these quiet spots are usually found where the shallows drop off rapidly into deep water near where a feeder stream enters the lake. They are often called ''holding'' areas by fisherfolk.

Another important factor in finding food has to do with the trouts' ability to see. Too little (or too much) light makes it difficult for them to distinguish a moving grub from a twig or pine needle. So fish will usually lurk at the depth of water that offers the right amount of light. They'll feed in shallow water in the early morning, then move deeper during the day, and feed again in the shallows at dusk.

What kind of food do trout look for in the spring? Mainly grubs. Some grubs float free; some squirm in the mud; many are encased in little ''houses'' of bark and sand. Open the stomach of a trout and you'll usually find a few partially digested grubs along with lots of dirt, twigs, and mud.

Occasionally the fish in these holding areas get a special treat, a batch of trout eggs or roe. Springtime marks egg-laying time for trout, and many females swim up into the feeder streams to deposit eggs in warmer, shallower water. The males just wait without eating in these shallow streambeds, ready to fertilize the eggs. Sometimes a batch is washed from its sandy bed and floats down to the lake. Lake trout are always watching for eggs in the springtime.

How should you fish mountain lakes in the spring? We usually cast fairly deep, near the inlet of a feeder stream, baiting with salmon eggs. Try to find the ''drop-off'' point and get your eggs just over the ledge. Late in the day, when the water is still warm and the light is losing its glare, those hungry fish will move toward your bait. Chances of a nibble are good.

If you're stream fishing, you can sometimes catch spawners in the shallow creek beds by drawing a lure in front of them—slowly, as if it were an intruder to their nesting area. The fish won't be hungry, but may grow angry and snap at it in order to protect their turf.

Summer: July And August

In early and mid-summer, the days turn long and hot in the mountains. The snow is gone; the creeks have slowed. The biggest change from springtime is the proliferation of insect life. Larvae emerge from their twig and sand houses, crawl into the sun on top of a rock, and metamorphose into small flies and bugs. Grasshoppers emerge from eggs and begin hopping through the grassy meadows.

The rushing, running water of the spring is gone. Insect life centers on and around the mountain lakes. Their surfaces become breeding grounds for insects too tiny to see. These in turn become food for larger flying insects which dance along the surface of the water whenever it is calm, eating the smaller ones. From the fish's eye view, the livin' is easy.

Trout continue to spawn during the early summer, with females swimming up feeder streams to lay. Many of the eggs laid earlier in spring now hatch. Shallow waters are filled with tiny trout, or minnows, which provide excellent nourishment for larger fish. The minnows soon learn the importance of remaining near shelter at all times.

In summer, the lake divides into 3 layers of water: an upper warm layer, a lower cold layer, and a combined middle layer. In the morning, the trout come into the shallows to feed on nymphs and minnows. The water here is cooler then and the low sun makes it easier to see the nymphs (larval flies which swim several inches below the surface of the water) and minnows, which hang out in nooks and crannies for protection.

During midday, the trout move lower, to cooler water. The brighter it gets, the deeper they go. They spend most of these hours nosing around the bottom for grubs, larval flies which live in the mud. Occasionally the fish come across some tasty fish eggs or a small worm. Then in the afternoon, they go back to the shallower areas to feed, primarily in the shade, where it is easier for them to see the surface.

During late afternoon, when the cold-blooded insects are most active on the water and sunlight strikes the lake at an angle, the trout will rise to work the surface. This is when you'll see the trout jumping. They wait below the still surface for a fly to land and feed. Then they come up — so fast that they just keep going, often completely out of the water. This is always a thrill to see and usually means it's the prime time to catch dinner.

Yet trout fishing any hour of the summertime day can be really pleasurable. In the morning we often fish with lures. Lures spin bright and silvery in the water, imitating minnows darting through the upper layers of the lake. During the middle of the day, the fish often seem to "stop biting." They've gone to the cooler depths to forage for grubs. Sometimes they can be caught with salmon eggs, but catching a tan is a better bet, or a nap in the shade after a swim while the old fishing rod, secured by a few sturdy rocks, takes care of itself. If the salmon eggs get soggy, so what?

Afternoons are the most productive times to fish. Everything seems to work. We fish flies when the trout are jumping. We fish lures

along the steep drop-offs, often following the shadow line along the shore, as the fish do underwater. We also fish with grasshoppers near the shore in shady places under overhanging bushes. These are the likely spots where grasshoppers may accidentally fall into the lake, spots where the fish will be waiting for them. This time of day usually gives us our memories and the best fish stories, and if things work out, a pan full of the freshest supper you could ever want.

Fall: September And Early October

In the fall, the water level is the year's lowest. The days get shorter, nights colder, food scarcer. The creeks and streams feeding the lakes have all but dried up. There isn't much insect life flowing through the lake. The temperature layers of the lake water begin to equalize.* As the surface water cools, it's easier for the trout to spend time in it.

At this time of year there are fewer but larger fish in the lakes. They are the survivors, and they want to fatten up for the winter cold spell. They feed on grubs and nymphs, now more plentiful in the shallower stretches, and on insects, which still land on the lake's surface in the late afternoon. Grasshoppers are fewer but fatter and still choice bait. Everything seems more tempting to the hungry fish.

---

*Water is densest, i.e. heaviest, at about 39 degrees F. When the surface water is cooled to 39, as it is in the fall with the night air close to freezing, it sinks to the bottom. The 3 layers of summer become one in the fall.

Fishing in the fall is thus similar to fishing in the summer—with one big exception: with the fish bigger and hungrier, and the action near or on the surface most of the day, it's even easier! There are a couple of other bonuses as well: the weather is better and the wilderness less crowded. Now if you could only arrange vacation time then....

Rivers And Streams

Stream fishing, like lake fishing, has its unique pleasures and problems. It promises more solitude—a chance to get off by yourself even near the trail; and while it's hard work it's often productive and usually satisfying, whether you bag a fish or not. Stream fishing means a lot of hiking for a little angling. It often requires hopping on rocks, or holding onto overhanging branches for dear life or taking off your pants and putting on your boots, or getting your line tangled in thickets of brush, or all the above. Yet the angler who is willing to fish a mountain stream often will return to camp with a string of trout, having discovered the right tackle and baits and the best places to fish only a spit and a holler from the well-worn path.

Many hiking trails parallel streams, dipping down occasionally to cross them at fordable points. At those points are often located well-used (and sometimes populated) campsites. But just a few hundred yards in either direction up or down stream, you'll find no sign of human life and often many signs of underwater life. A little scrambling gets you a lot of fishing. And if the fish aren't biting, you can retrace your steps, hike along the trail, leave it again where it approaches the stream, and continue for a whole day, covering long stretches of running water. Along the way you'll often discover several natural, picture-perfect campsites, too remote for the casual hiker. There you can set up shop for a couple days of fine early morning and late afternoon fishing.

Stream trout eat the same things as lake trout, but they tend to secure their food in a different way. By knowing what, how, and where they eat, you can usually find and often catch them. Larvae, grubs, insects, eggs and minnows thrive in streams as well as lakes and fill up the "market basket" of hungry river fish. Your job is to figure out just what the fish are feeding on—you may have to try several riggings and baits before you get the right one—and then go after them. Here's how.

Lake trout, you remember, move around looking for food. River trout, conversely, stay in one place. That's the major difference between the two and makes for a different kind of fishing. As the river water flows, it carries insects, eggs, larvae with it. A fish needn't move to get the food when food is moving to it. This is ecological efficiency at work, and by tapping into its logic, you can imitate nature with your bait and catch a fish.

The fish has to know where the food is coming from and where to be to get it. Obviously it'll come from upstream. The place to be, if you're a stream trout, is in a quiet pool well protected from danger and just off the mainstream which carries the goodies along. Such pools may be under an overhanging boulder, bank, or branch, beneath a rotted log, or at the bend of the river where the flow eddies wide, leaving a quiet spot near one bank. They may be at the far end of a rapids or beneath a miniature waterfall or cascade, all of which act as natural conveyor belts for the food that fish want.

Stream trout "hold" in these pools (hence the angling term, "holding pools"), and watch the rapidly flowing main current without having to swim against it. When a morsel flows by, they dart out and grab it. Then it's back to the safety of the shadowed pool to watch and wait for more of the same. Like the fish, you can also trace the path of the food. Toss a leaf into the flowing stream or over the cascade. See how it's taken by the current into a calmer spot: that's the pool. Now try to cast your baited hook in such a way that it does the same thing as the leaf. Throw your bait into the current. The eggs, if that's what you're using, will sink slightly, then be carried into the pool below. If you've done your homework, and fish are waiting, you'll get a quick bite. River fish are not likely to mouth the bait and spit it out several times as lake fish often do. River fish must get their food on the first bite or watch it disappear downstream.

Several casts like this, allowing the bait to flow into the pool, are all you need. Change baits if you like, to see if something else works. No bite means no fish. Look around for other likely holding pools nearby. Perhaps there's a log blocking the current, creating a pool. A fish might lurk behind it, observing the water flow by. Let your bait drift past. Still no bites? Then it's time to move on.

Moving on takes some care. You need to be quiet and cautious at the same time — quiet in order to sneak up on fish which are often merely a foot below the surface, and cautious to keep from slipping, tripping, falling along overgrown banks and slippery rocks. River trout are easily spooked. Once they see your shadow or are startled by rocks and gravel you set in motion as you pratfall upstream, they're likely to duck into a safe hiding place for hours.

Once you manage to get to the holding pools without sending all the fish to the local fright-recovery unit, and if you have the right bait, your chances of landing a trout are greatly enhanced if you fish early or late in the day. When there's little light on the water, the fish see the surface better and, like their lake cousins, go for living foods on or just below it. At midday, they go as deep as they can, still watching the flowing water for an easy lunch in the deep shade. You might try it yourself.

One last thing. To quiet and caution, add patience. Stream fishing can be frustrating. Your line can get snagged on an overhanging branch, the hook or lure can get hung up on a submerged rock or log, the trout on your line can free himself by taking your line under a rock and snapping it. But the rewards of solitude, beauty, challenge, and good eating more than make up for the hard parts. Take it slow, easy, and enjoy.

Arrows indicate "holding pools," where stream trout can sit and watch for edibles flowing past with the current

Fishing In The Rain

When rain clouds roll in on summer afternoons, many campers head into their tents. *We* put on ponchos and parkas, and head out to fish. Some of our most memorable fishing has been on rainy afternoons.

One theory has it that fish can't possibly conceive of any other creature, especially an over-coddled human, who might prefer to be as wet as they are. Thus, when they see a shiny lure dancing through the rain-splashed water, they figure it's the real thing. Our theory doesn't attribute quite so much intelligence to the trout. We've found that as the storm moves in, the fish stop biting. They sense the air pressure decreasing—what weather forecasters mean by the barometer falling. Fish—and most other living things—seek shelter.

Once the storm is in full splendor, the barometer steadies, then begins to rise. As the air pressure increases, the rain may still be falling, but the fish sense that the worst is over, and out they go to see what fresh food has entered the lake. The rain washes the surface of the lake clean; new bugs, appearing on the surface, are likely to be alive; minnows darting below the surface are likely to be real; and anglers' shadows, broken by the rain-mottled surface, are likely to go unnoticed. While all this is conjecture, the fact is that if you don't mind the wet, fishing in the rain can be highly successful and a lot more fun than huddling in the tent.

Gear

Mountain trout are usually small. Most range from 8-12 inches in length and weigh a little under a pound. A 2-3 pounder in the high country is a monster. And even these require very little in the way of gear to bait, hook, and reel into your frying pan.

First, you need a rod and reel. We leave fancy fly fishing, with its graphite rods, hand-tied flies and special line, to the purists. Instead, we use a simple telescoping spinning rod. It telescopes down to a 2-foot length, short enough to stick in the backpack, though it's also long and stiff enough to give a good cast. Inexpensive models can even be found in some drugstores. But treat them gently and pack them carefully: expensive or cheap, they're fragile.

Reels come in all shapes and sizes. A look at *Consumer Reports* might be in order before you put your money down. The more expensive reels have better machinery inside—bearings, gears and levers—that last longer and take more abuse. The cheaper "backpacking" reels are lighter, less substantial and more likely to jam up after you drop them onto the ground or into the sand a couple of times. We usually compromise—the best combination of inexpensive and lightweight that our discount sports store has in stock when we're buying.

If you're left-handed, you might want a left-handed reel which permits you to wind in with your right hand while holding the rod and reel in your left. On the other hand (!), you might want to learn to fish with a righty's reel. It isn't hard and saves bringing extra gear if you don't mind sharing.

It's a good idea to practice taking the cover off the reel and lubricating the inside mechanism. It won't take many trips before your reel falls into the water or sand for one reason or another. If you don't lubricate it soon afterwards, certainly before your next outing, it will get sticky and much harder to cast properly. For this purpose, you can either buy a special reel lubricant or use any light gear-and-bearing grease.

You'll need fishing line on the reel. We usually deposit our reels at a local bait and tackle shop a few days before each outing and have them wound with 4 pound monofilament line. The shop has a special winding machine which lays the line on evenly and regularly.

If you prefer, you can wind the line onto the spool yourself. Set up the rod and reel as if you were going fishing. Thread the line through the rod's eyelets and tie it to the spool of the reel with the bail open. Drop the spool of fresh line into a clean waste basket. Grasp the line and rod with your right hand about a foot up from the reel. Snap the bail shut and reel the new line in with your left hand. Keep a slight drag on the line with your right hand, and watch the reel as you wind. If you see

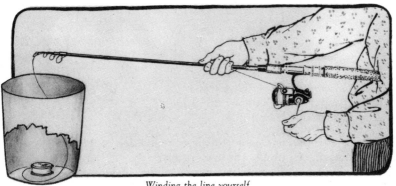

Winding the line yourself.

stray loops or uneven winding, vary the drag until you get it right. Don't allow any lumps, clumps, twirls or snags to grow on the spool. Be sure the line lays down in even symmetrical rows.

Why do you need fresh line each outing? The monofilament tends to shape itself to the spool on which it's wound. Line which has been on your reel for several months tends to lie in the water in hundreds of little curlicues. As you reel in these curls, they quickly form hundreds of small knots. Then you spend your fishing time untangling knots instead of casting—a disheartening task.

The rest of your backpacking fishing tackle, except for a net, should fit easily into a large Ziploc bag. In that bag, supplies should be divided into smaller bags or plastic boxes. It's important both to save weight when backpacking and to save space in the pack. Don't fill your fishing bag with empty space. Pack lightly but efficiently.

Basically, you'll need the following items:

• *Flies.* A dozen small flies will fit into a tiny bag, box, or foam-lined case. Buy various colors and shapes, with hook sizes between 8 and 14. Most of our flies are on #10 or #12 hooks. They cost between 50 cents and a dollar each, though hand-tied flies will set you back a lot more.

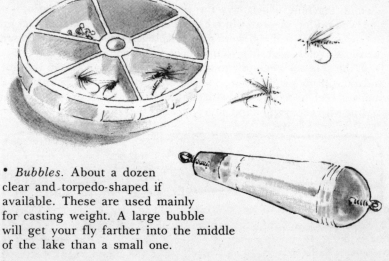

• *Bubbles.* About a dozen clear and torpedo-shaped if available. These are used mainly for casting weight. A large bubble will get your fly farther into the middle of the lake than a small one.

• *Hooks.* One package each of hooks already tied to a small piece of leader, sizes 8, 10, 12, 14. The leaders have a loop at the other end and can be clipped easily onto a snap or swivel in your rigging.

• *Spare Line.* We usually bring 100 yards of 4-pound test monofilament on a spool. This can be wound directly onto your reel if you run completely out, (as a result, for example, of having consecutively cut away tangled sections). Spare line can also be used as "leader"—line tied directly to a fly or bait. Some people bring 25 yards of 2-pound test monofilament to use as leader.

• *Snaps.* About 30 of the smallest you can find. These are used at the end of the line to attach bubbles, lures and other riggings.

• *Swivels.* About 10, all small. These attach weights or hooks in the middle of a rigging. They can be 2- or 3-way swivels. They are helpful in dreaming up new ways to rig your bait.

• *Weights.* Two packages (20 weights each) of 1/8 oz. "egg sinkers." These are sliding weights with a hole down the middle. Also, one package of 1/4 oz. egg sinkers for long-distance, deep water casts.

• *Lures.* About a dozen lures with treble (triple) hooks, sizes 8, 10, 12. This will allow you to lose a few and still have a reserve. Lures have a habit of snagging; you'll donate quite a number to the lake or stream bottom. The larger, heavier lures can be cast farther. Smaller, lighter lures work better in mountain streams; they don't sink as fast so they're less likely to snag on sunken trees and branches. Check with your favorite expert about his or her special lure before you shop—lures are expensive. We've had the most success with 1½ Super Dupers and ½ oz. (#6) Panther Martins.

- *Salmon Eggs*. Two small bottles of Pautchke's "Balls of Fire," Green label. This brand is slightly more expensive but comes highly recommended. Keep the eggs in their glass bottles despite the excess weight. Also keep them cool and in the shade or they'll start to spoil.
- *Net*. Get the smallest, lightest net available from a tackle shop. Pack it with the pots, pans and plates and it'll add very little weight and take up hardly any space. It helps a lot in landing fish, especially from a steep, rocky shore.
- *License*. You might never meet a ranger or game warden in the backcountry who wants to see your license, but you need one anyway. The fee is steep but worth it, and your money goes to a good cause. It's used by your state's Fish and Game people to restock lakes, maintain hatcheries, and keep streams and rivers clear. Don't travel without one. And make sure, when you get one, to pick up a free copy of your state's fishing regulations. It explains what kind of fishing is legal in which areas at what times of year. Read carefully.

Baits and Riggings

The best way to find out if "they're biting" and "what to use" is to ask those who are there or who you meet on the trail coming from your lake. If they tell you, "Salmon eggs toward the lake inlet," go to it with salmon eggs. If they tell you, "Lures by the steep north wall," don't use flies by the inlet. That's simple enough.

Of course, this presumes the presence of people with information. The farther off the beaten track, the fewer ready-made answers. Alone at a lake, deciding what and where to fish becomes a wonderful challenge. Size up the lake closely for a few moments. Where does the water come in? Where does it leave? Where are the deepest spots? Where are the shady overhangs? Consider the season, the weather, and the time of day to figure out where the fish might be.

If you prepare wisely, you're ready in advance for any kind of fishing, deep or shallow, lures or bait. Your lures, fastened to a cork in your tackle bag so they won't tangle, can clip easily onto the snap at the end of the line. Your salmon-egg rigging is tied up inside a small plastic bag, available for instant use. If the fish are jumping in the shady section of the lake, you can quickly switch from eggs to a bubble and fly. Or perhaps you feel like putting a grasshopper in the water near the shrubs by the base of a steep cliff, then reading another chapter of your book as you wait for a tug on the line. It's fun and easy to experiment when you've put your riggings together in advance; it's frustrating when that big cahoonga is right there laughing at you, as you try to tie new knots, re-rig a line, and catch a grasshopper at the same time.

Fishing Knots, Swivels And Clips

Like Boy Scouts, anglers often wallow lovingly in the intricacies of knotsmanship. ''Lark's head loops'' and ''Bimini twists'' are often cited as prerequisites to catching large fish. Fortunately this is not the case. Everything in your fishing arsenal can be tied strongly and securely with a simple square knot, and confusion about the fancier systems of connecting line and tackle won't prevent your catching a single trout. Nevertheless, for the precision angler and other fine-tuners, we include on the next few pages a few simple knots and tying instructions. We often use the clinch knot.

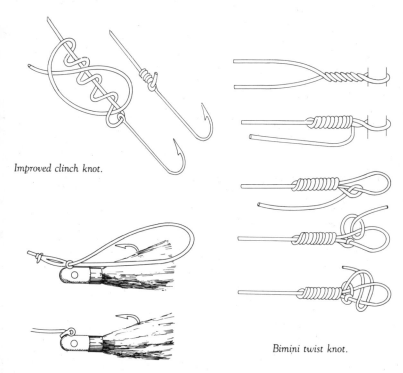

Improved clinch knot.

Bimini twist knot.

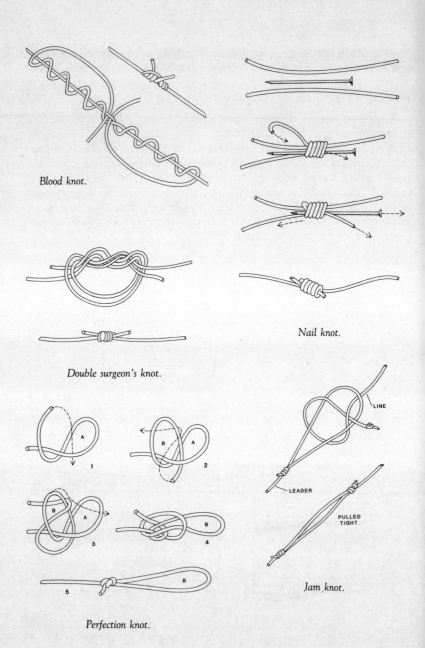

Blood knot.

Nail knot.

Double surgeon's knot.

Perfection knot.

Jam knot.

Swivels are used to tie one piece of tackle to another so they won't slip or come apart. For example, when you fish with salmon eggs, you may want 2 groups of eggs suspended above the bottom of the lake. A couple of 3-way swivels allow you to connect 2 short "drop" leaders to the main line with a minimum of fuss (See Illustration, p. 119).

A snap at the end of the line is a must; it'll save you a lot of time when you're making up and changing riggings. You can clip a lure onto the end of your line for fishing deep. Then, if the fish start feeding on surface insects, you can easily detach that lure to clip on a bubble and fly rigging. Snaps save you from cutting the line and retying whenever you change tackle. Remember, early morning and evening are the times when it will be most difficult for you to see the line to tie or untangle it; yet those are the times of the most fishing action. If you have a supply of snaps and swivels in your tackle bag, you'll be ready for those quick changes when time counts.

Salmon Egg Riggings

Salmon eggs are usually rigged for deep fishing during times when no fish surface to feed. These riggings are also good for any other bait which isn't supposed to be alive: a bit of salami or scrap of cheese, for example. You want to get these bits of food to where the fish are — along the bottom looking for food that has been washed into the lake. Trout lay eggs in clusters; if they wash away from the shallow stream in which they were laid, they remain clustered as they're carried down into the lake. We usually stick 3 or 4 salmon eggs on a #8 hook to simulate nature. One hint on getting them to stay hooked: lay them in the sun about 15 minutes before you use them. This hardens the outside skin and makes them less likely to float off the hook.

When a lake trout spots a cluster of salmon eggs, it will often mouth them, not swallowing them completely at first. Our first suggested rigging is called the Long Lake Rigging (after the lake where two old-timers taught it to us). It suspends 2 clusters of eggs several inches above the lake bottom. When you feel a slight tug on the line, wait just a moment, then "set" the hook in the trout's mouth by pulling up a bit on the rod. The point is to try to snag the fish's lip as it's drawing the bait in for a second mouthing. If you don't wait, you'll pull up empty, for the fish will have let the bait go before taking another taste. With this rigging, you need to hold the line fairly taut at all times so you're sensitive to what's happening at the other end.

Our other suggestion is called the Grizzly Lake Rigging. It rests the bait down on the lake bed and depends on a hungry trout to gobble it up completely. The fish won't know the eggs are on a hook until they're in

Long Lake Rigging.

Grizzly Lake Rigging.

its stomach. It's a perfect rigging for reading, sunning, napping, even cooking. You cast, lean the rod against a rock or your leg, and wait. The line goes slack. The fish feels no resistance as it mouths the bait and pulls back, because the line feeds freely through the doughnut weight. When you feel or see a tug on the slack line, the hook is already set, and the fish is ready to be reeled in.

With either rigging, the weight should be only as heavy as necessary to get the hook(s) and salmon eggs where you want them. Heavy weights may cast farther, but as soon as a fish bites, that heavier weight gives the trout an advantage. All it has to do is go rapidly in one direction—up, for example—then switch directions with a snap of its head. If the weight is heavy enough, the line will break. Though the fish still has a hook in its mouth, you'll reel in an empty line. We usually start with eighth- or quarter-ounce sinkers and #8 hooks, whatever the rigging.

Any rigging meant to lie on the lake bottom tends to snag as you reel it in. Leave the rigging motionless for several minutes after you cast, so it may settle free of an obstruction that might otherwise snag it immediately. After that, a twitch every few minutes won't hurt and might attract a fish to the moving eggs. When you're ready to cast from a different rock or in another direction, pick up the line quickly from the lake bottom by reeling it in fast. *Keep* reeling fast so the hooks and sinker stay above sharp rocks and dead tree trunks on the bottom of the lake.

Bubble-And-Fly Rigging

The evening is warm, the air still, the lake calm, the surface of the water broken only by the fish jumping for insects. If you're equipped to simulate the insects you'll almost certainly get a fish. That's where the bubble-and-fly come in.

This rigging consists of a fly tied onto one end of several feet of leader, either 4 lb. or 2 lb. test line, and a teardrop bubble tied on the other. The bubble's weight lets you cast the fly where the fish are feeding. Once the bubble-and-fly land, the object is to make the fly seem like all those other surface bugs. Watch how the real flies behave; you'll see them scooting across the water close to shore. Reel in the line with quick short bursts so the fly seems to dart along like its real-life cousins.

The best thing about bubble-and-fly fishing is that you rarely have to worry about snags. You can spend your time casting and retrieving rather than losing masses of tackle on underwater branches. Once in a while you'll snag a fly on a bush when fishing near shore; also, be care-

ful of trees and shrubs on your backswing. But if you develop good casting habits, you'll while away the hours snagging fish rather than unsnagging line.

Flies come in a wide variety of shapes, sizes and colors. When the fish are jumping in those out-of-the-way backcountry lakes, neither shape nor color seem to matter. Size, however, is important. The fish are small; so are the bugs they eat. Try sizes 10 or 12. We've also noticed that flies produce the best results when they're first cast. They hit the water dry, and sit on the surface for the first several casts. Thereafter they ride slightly below the surface, and the fish are a little less likely to go after them. Sometimes we whip the fly through the air several times between casts in order to dry it off.

Keep moving as you fish bubble-and-fly. After a half-dozen casts in one area or direction, walk on. You can cover a whole lake this way, perfecting your casting technique, seeing the site from startling new perspectives, and, if the fish are feeding, bagging dinner into the bargain. We backpack with a number of fanatics who don't care if they ever catch a fish. They just love the feel of casting, and over the years have become expert at placing the fly a micrometer's distance from an overhanging branch, an inaccessible inlet, a rocky spit. Now, if we could just get them to move where the fish are...

Fishing With Lures

The bigger the trout, the more likely it is to feed on small fish. From the backpacker's point of view, a lure is the closest thing to fishing with small fish; it often gets you the biggest trout. A lure is bright, shiny, silvery, often spoon-shaped. It dances and flashes throught the water, reflecting light much like a minnow. Lure fishing requires a technique simulating the movements of a tiny fish—darting quickly, stopping momentarily, darting again. The art is in the play of the line, not in the distance of the cast, which can be quite short. As in bubble-and-fly fishing, you have to keep moving—your lure and yourself. If you're fishing a stream, don't let the lure sink very far or you'll end up with a rock on the end of your line.

If trout are feeding on smaller fish, they have to move fast when they see one. The speedy minnow will try to hide instantly, if it senses danger. It can dart into areas too shallow for the big guys; it can escape under logs or into holes beneath banks. So quickness is essential, for both minnow and trout; as soon as a trout sees the minnow flashing in the water, it strikes. The lure is below the surface; you can't see what's happening. If you feel a nibble, you've usually hooked the fish, because it hits the triple-barbed hook with mouth wide open, intent on swallowing the small fish whole. One minute you're reeling in the lure; the next you've got a big trout solid on the line.

Suppose the large fish aren't feeding on minnows. They may still be attracted by the lure. They often swim up and seem to check it out, following it toward shore. If they're cautious, their senses will alert them that the lure doesn't sound or smell like a minnow; they'll move away. It's an angler's nightmare to watch the big one follow a lure up to shore without biting. But frustration goes with the franchise, just as excitement does, and if that fish lives to savor a real minnow today, he'll be there for the taking tomorrow.

Another problem with lures is that they're made to fish deeper than flies. They ride somewhere between 6 inches and 2 feet below the surface as you reel them in; you can't see what's happening so it's harder to direct their path. Most lures have a 3-pronged hook, which is more likely to catch a trout's mouth, but also more likely to snag underwater weeds or branches. Furthermore, if you have a problem with your equipment while the lure is in the water, the moment you stop reeling the treble hook drifts downward to catch on whatever lies there. By the time you fix the reel or untangle the line, the lure is hopelessly hooked on the lake bottom. One thing about lure fishing: it's never dull.

Fishing With Grasshoppers

An old saying goes, "You can catch any fish if you've got the right bait." Natural bait stimulates all the fish's senses. It's the r-e-e-a-l thing. Grasshoppers are a special treat to lake trout, and depending on the time of day and year, fish will be attuned to the possibility of a large hopper falling onto the lake's surface. Not only will a trout go after one without hesitation, it will often encounter fierce competiton from kindred fish for the tasty tidbit.

The challenge of capturing the grasshoppers themselves, however, more than makes up for the ease of landing the fish that bites the hopper that feeds it. There are whole books on the subject; well, chapters anyway. One suggests chasing hoppers onto a blanket: they get stuck in the blanket hairs and are easy pickin'. Plausible, but not many backpackers carry wool blankets into the high country anymore. Another expert calls for an insect net, also a great idea if you're not backpacking. We have our own methods, summed up by the rueful phrase, "going to great lengths." The bare-handed stab is the classiest technique, though it helps if you're The Flash. Those bugs move fast! The pot-lid slam is inelegant, often resulting in a dented pot lid and a handful of meadow, while the hopper easily eludes this oafish lunge. Our favorite exercise in futility, however, is the "long-distance pole press" invented one morning by Rick as he wandered forlornly through an Eden of grasshoppers with a fishing rod in hand. The long, narrow pole, he noticed, casts only a thin shadow which hoppers don't seem to notice. Once the pole is directly over its victim, you bring it down suddenly, pinning the hopper on the ground. Sometimes instead of pinning the hopper, this artful action stuns it, so you can pick it up while it's still dazed from the blow. Sometimes, instead of stunning the bug, you kill it, which is great if you're fighting a plague of locusts but not so good if you're trying to look like an expert. And sometimes—often, in Hal's case—you miss the grasshopper altogether. That pole is limber, and requires a modicum of hand-eye coordination. No matter how you try, it ain't easy.

Spring meadows are often literally covered with baby grasshoppers, and the catching's easier. As the year moves on, the hopper population decreases and the adults have more savvy. Like all insects, grasshoppers are cold-blooded. Dependent on the sun's warmth for their energy, they are least active in the morning, and thus theoretically there for the picking, right off leaves and grasses with your fingers. The only trouble in practice is that you can't see them till they flee, always just out of reach, and then you're back to square one: Cunning Strategies.

Some hoppers have wings and fly each time they take off; some just hop. The key to catching them is to sneak up from behind, thus avoiding their field of vision which extends roughly from the middle of their right side to the middle of their left. They'll jump just as your hand comes even with their heads, but not before. Try to move your hand slowly into position, perhaps one inch behind the hopper. Be careful not to cast a shadow on it as you move. Then suddenly slap down your open palm. Come down hard, quick and flat: splat! Usually, you won't kill the hopper; even if you do the fish won't care. Twelve-year-olds have an uncanny ability to catch grasshoppers this way.

Once you catch enough hoppers, you can keep them alive for as long as 2 days in a sealed plastic bag. Store them in the shade and be careful not to crush them at the bottom of your pack.

Hopper fishing is done with a rigging similar to a bubble-and-fly. The only difference is that the hook is empty. When you're ready to cast, poke the sharp point of the hook into the underside of the hopper's neck and out again at the belly-button. The hopper will stay alive for a short while because its head hasn't been damaged. It may even flutter its wings in the water, attracting the fish.

Hooking a hopper

The best place to fish hoppers is under the overhanging limb of a bush or tree where a hopper would be likely to fall in, or where the fish are already jumping. Sometimes when all else fails—the flies and lures and eggs—a hopper will save the day and provide your evening's dining pleasure. They're worth the scramble.

Casting And Reeling

Nothing is more satisfying than catching trout in the wilderness. Nothing is more peaceful and relaxing than the routine of casting and retrieving a lure or fly, working the lake surface in the late afternoon while the fish feed. And nothing is more frustrating than snagging a lure or tangling your line because of improper reeling. The blood boils as your line becomes hopelessly tangled just when the fishing would be most rewarding. The sun is setting, the fish are jumping, and there you are, on your hands and knees trying to untangle a seemingly endless number of knots while your lure drifts slowly toward the lake floor to snag on a hidden log or brush. It makes you want to cry.

Prevent this by developing and practicing good casting habits—in the local park at home or at the campsite using only a bubble on the line. Grip the rod as shown in the illustration (p. 130). Point it in the diretion you intend to cast. Catch the line on the ball of your forefinger. Then open the bail. With one smooth motion bring the tip of the rod up, just past vertical, then back down. As the rod passes the "10 o'clock" position in front of you, straighten your forefinger. The line will spin off the reel as it follows the bubble across the lake. Once the bubble or lure is in the water, give the handle on the reel a quick turn to snap the bail back into position. As you continue turning the handle, the line reels regularly and neatly onto the spool, ready to peel off with little resistance on the next cast.

Hold the line with your forefinger, raise the rod just past vertical, then cast. As the tip passes "10 o'clock," let go of the line

Reeling in the line seems simple, but requires some vigilance at the beginning. Most backpacking reels are small and light; the line is wound in very small loops around a narrow spool. When the line shoots out over the water, it pulls straighter at the bubble end than it does near the reel. The line on the water near you will be twirled and curled; when you begin to reel in, it might tangle itself into a knot. And even a small knot on the line will foul up smooth casting.

To prevent these tangles, you need to watch the line as you reel in the first 10 or 15 feet. This is distracting: your attention is usually focused where the fish are. Force yourself. Watch for knots and tangles until the line is straight in the water.

Another way to lick tangles is to grasp the rod and line with your rod hand about a foot in front of the reel as you begin to haul in. As the line slips through your hand, you'll feel any knots and can untangle them on the spot.

What if you reel in a tangle or knot without noticing it? The first indication will be a sudden halt to your lure or bubble as you cast. Knots and tangles catch in the eyelets through which the line passes along the rod. This will stop your cast dead. Then you'll have to decide whether to untangle the mess or just cut it off and continue with the fresh line still on your spool. Most spools contain about 3 times the amount of line you actually use when casting. If you cut off a length of tangled mess, you'll still have enough for an afternoon's fishing. If you have to cut again, however, you'll be approaching the end of what line is on the reel. Once you hit the bottom of the spool, you'll need to wind on new line, either from the extra 4 lb. monofilament in your fishing bag, or from another reel (see above for instructions on winding line onto an empty spool).

What happens if you're in a wooded area where branches are too close to permit an overhead cast? Use a side-arm cast. Practice casting *from* either side *to* either side. That way, you'll be prepared to fight your way through brush and cast from a muddy bank overgrown with dense bushes. You can still put the lure or bubble wherever you want it.

Underwater Snags

Try as you might, the line will occasionally snag underwater. First make sure you haven't actually caught a large fish! The big ones sometimes move so slowly you might mistake them for a rock. Watch the line carefully in the water as you hold it tight. If it moves at all, it's a fish! Otherwise, you've got a snag. Don't just snap a snagged line. Try loosening its tension and pulling again from all directions; walk back and forth along the bank, hop around the rocks. You may get lucky and dislodge it. If the weather is warm and the water not too cold, you can swim out to free it. Sometimes we cut the line and tie it somewhere on shore; in the heat of the following day, we'll screw up our nerve, jump in, and retrieve the lure.

If you decide to sacrifice the lure or rigging, be careful not to snap your rod while snapping the line. Point the rod in the direction of the snagged lure. Wrap the line 2 or 3 times around your hand between the reel and the first eyelet on the rod. (If your skin cuts easily, wrap the line around your shirtsleeve near your wrist. The line, when taut, is knife-like.) Then walk backward. The line will normally break near the lure, though sometimes the extra pressure will free the lure from the snag. Either way, when the line suddenly goes limp, reel it in. Never try to snap a line by raising the tip of the rod. That's guaranteed to break the rod instead.

Playing And Landing A Trout

What's A Drag?

When a fish takes your hook, it reacts like any animal with something sharp and painful in its mouth—it flees as rapidly and strongly as it can away from this danger toward a secure hiding place. At this point, it's up to you to "play" the fish, to let it run against constant resistance, to tire it out.

If your line is taut, the fish might snap it with a few quick maneuvers. How can a one-pound fish snap a "4-pound test" line? Easy. The "4-pound" figure indicates only the amount of dead, motionless weight the line can lift vertically off the ground. Even a one-pound fish moving rapidly exerts more than 4 pounds of force on a taut line. When it does, the line will snap.

Spinning reels are equipped with a "drag" to prevent this. This drag adjustment allows the line to unwind when it's pulled hard by a fish; that is, it unwinds rather than snaps. Check and adjust the drag each time you fish. Don't wait till the fish hits your lure or bait. You may not have time.

The drag is adjusted with the same screw mechanism that holds the spool in position on the reel. Most inexpensive backpacking reels economize with a cheap drag adjustment. The vibration of the reel winding and unwinding, the snapping of the bail, even the bouncing of your pack as you hike can disturb the drag mechanism, and you'll need to fiddle with it from time to time.

First check the adjustment. Grab the line below the closed reel and pull. The line should go taut; then the spool should begin to revolve, allowing line to peel off. If you can pull hard enough to snap the line without it unwinding, the drag's too tight. If there's no resistance, it's too loose. Adjusted right, a solid tug will unwind the line slowly against a constant resistance. Remember that a very small change in the adjustment nut—1/8 or 1/4 of a turn—will make all the difference in the drag. Make sure to check it each time you fish.

If, when you test the drag, the handle and bail revolve so line comes easily off the spool, the reel's one-way-only ratcheting mechanism is not engaged. It's controlled by a little lever or switch on the reel. It should always be engaged when you fish, so the reel makes a soft clicking sound as you wind the line in.

Landing Fish

If a fish gets away while you're trying to land it, it's usually because your heart is working faster than your head. Finally, after all that waiting and all that work, you've got a live, furious creature on the end of a pathetically thin line, and there are too many things to do all at the same time. The rod is bobbing and weaving, your friends are cheering,

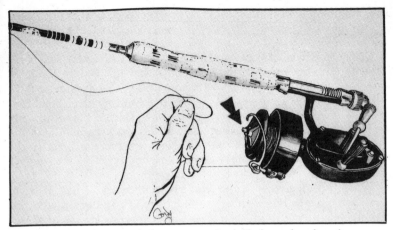

Adjust the drag with the same screw that holds the spool on the reel.

whooping and being useless with a million suggestions, none of which you can hear for all the pounding inside your ears. It feels like you're waltzing with a tiger and he knows all the steps.

OK. Try to remain cool and collected; that's part of the challenge. Besides, you want to *land* that thunderbolt. Adjust the drag as you begin to play the fish. Bring it closer. Make it work, pulling against the drag, taking the line slowly out. Then increase the drag a touch and reel it in again. The fish is now close enough to see. It's a big one! Dinner for four! Better repeat the process. Let it go out now; reel it in another time. Is it still fighting mad? Do it again! Don't try to land a biggy until it's tired. Otherwise you'll end up discussing dinner rather than eating it.

The big ones are heart stoppers, but the small ones are exhilarating too. And most of the fish you'll catch in the mountains will be small — in the 8-10 inch bracket: great eating and easy to store. Bring the small fry close to shore, then lift it out of the water and away from the lake in one fluid motion. If you decide to release the fish — it may be *too* small or you may only be fishing for sport — get the hook out of the fish's mouth as quickly and gently as possible. Then hold it lightly in your hand and place it under the surface of the water. If it has enough strength to survive, it will dart quickly away with a sudden, swift motion. If it's nearly dead, it will float motionless in your hand. Don't leave the fish floating if it has no strength to swim away. It's as good as dead, and there's no sense polluting the lake. Keep it and eat it.

Be careful about regulations on fish size. In some places, there's a legal minimum limit on the size of fish you can keep; smaller ones must be returned to the water. Check your regulation manual for this information.

The most efficient way to land a larger fish is with a net. This is absolutely imperative if, like us, you enjoy wading out into hip-deep water as you fish. Trying to grab a trout with bare hands is more difficult than catching the proverbial greased pig. Net your catch head-first so it moves *into* the net while trying to escape. Once it's in, lift the net out of the water; with your other hand, frimly grab the middle of the fish and webbing from the outside. Now remove the hook (while holding your rod out of the water, if necessary; it can be done), and release the fish or store it for later eating.

What if you don't have a net? You'll have to beach the fish. Keep in mind, when you do this, that fish fight harder as water gets shallower. Play the fish till it's tired, then lead it up to a sandy stretch of shore. With a single, continuous motion, guide the fish onto the beach. Don't jerk the line or it may break. Just pull steadily and the trout will follow. The fish might twitch and jump when it feels the sand, but if it's tired and your motion is swift and smooth, it won't realize what is happening until it's too late.

What if you have no net *and* no shore? When fishing from a rocky bank, you'll have to use the "clean and jerk" method. If the fish is tired and the water is shallow, use the same motion you would to beach a fish by pulling it out of the water toward land. Once it's airborne and moving in your direction, it may arch its body and wriggle frantically, or otherwise unhook itself or snap the line. Hopefully it has enough inertia at this point to continue shoreward and land on the rocky bank— flipping, flopping and unhooked but far enough from the water to prevent a last minute leap from the frying pan to the watery deep.

You've landed your fish and, like Rick with his 16-inch Golden trout, you need time to come down. Savor the moment and all your future bragging rights. Then put the gear in order (the line may be a mess), pack up the plastic bags, and head for the campsite, with your catch and a gleam in your eye that spells baked trout (and a loaf of bread) hot out of the "oven" for supper.

Cleaning And Storing Fish

Unless you're a pelican or a down-at-the-heels samurai, you'll want to clean your fish before eating it—an easy task. Ideally you should do it as soon after your catch as possible, but that's often impossible. You may be on a dayhike, or out in the raft, or too busy catching more to leave the lake and clean the one you've just caught. In those cases, stow the fish is a Ziploc bag or a pot, or thread it on a stick. Try to keep the fish out of the sun.

Fish are easy to clean, but it's also easy to foul the environment while doing it. Nothing is more depressing than to look into a lake or stream and see fish entrails floating around. *Always* clean fish far from all fresh water sources — and from your campsite. Don't even begin to clean them until you've found a spot with soft soil or sand and have dug a hole or trench at least 4 or 5 inches deep with your heel or a cup. That's going to be your Dispos-All.

To clean a fish, you need a sharp knife and some rinse water. Hold the fish in your hand, belly up. Slit the belly from the vent (the small hole just in front of the back fin) to just behind the head. If you plan to cut off the head (lots of folks leave it on), do so now. Cut on a diagonal line from just behind the front fins through to the spinal column. The fish is slippery; hold on tight. But that backbone is tough, so take care you don't take your hand off along with the head as the sharp knife severs the bone.

The fish is now opened. Most of the entrails will spill out on their own (into the hole). Remove the remainder with your hand, scraping away the tissue along the backbone with a thumb nail or knife. That's it! Rinse the cavity, put the fish in a bag or pot, clean your knife and hands, pour out the dirty rinse water, cover the hole and head for supper.

Fish are best cooked and eaten immediately after catching and cleaning. But this too is not always possible. To store cleaned fish overnight, keep them in a plastic bag inside a pot. You don't need any water. Cover the pot and set a heavy rock on it to discourage late, four-legged diners. The cold night air will preserve the fish and breakfast will be great.

CHAPTER VII:
Cooking & Eating

Hidden Lake Souffle

"Catch, clean and poach 3 to 5 small (7-9") trout taken from a crystalline wilderness lake at 8,000 feet." Thus reads the first sentence of our original recipe for Hidden Lake Souffle. "Remove and discard bones and skin. Set aside the flaked meat in tent to protect from flies, bees and larger predators. Over a low fire, prepare about a Sierra cup-and-a-half of white sauce in the smallest of a set of 3 nested pots. Do not eat ingredients halfway through. Assuage munchies or lingering hunger with dried fruit, nuts, candy, whatever, thus preserving the fish, cheese and eggs for the souffle. Add flaked fish to sauce, season well, and pour into a greased, two-quart pot. Fold in egg whites which have been beaten stiff with the trusty spring-loaded swizzle stick. Cover pot and bake in coals until done. Cooking time: one chapter of *Huckleberry Finn* read aloud. Eat at once. Bask in glow of self-congratulation. Groan with pleasure.''

We made up these directions one glorious morning in a remote campsite deep in the mountains. We'd planned the souffle as a late brunch, but the project built slowly and turned into an early dinner. That didn't matter. We had all the time in the world. This wasn't survival, it was hedonism, like a day trip, a long nap, or an hour of fly-casting at sundown. After dinner, we revised the recipe, wrote it out, and then, the next day, left it in a cairn atop an unnamed peak in the mountains. We don't know if anyone ever found it or tried to use it. We were told later, however, by friends who did try, that they needed something a bit more specific, and in the following pages we will take you step-by-step through this recipe (poaching, making a sauce, and baking) as well as through others that have kept us full and happy during long days in the mountains.

At the same time, though, we're trying to hook you on a general philosophy of backcountry cooking: with some basic knowledge and ingredients, you can concoct masterpieces in the wilderness. Recipes are fine in the beginning. You can jot some down in indelible ink on a few cards covered with plastic wrap that will fit into your map pouch. But the fact is, you don't need any. Here's how to improvise, how to play variations on simple themes, how to work from the general to the specific: how to have your cake and eat it too!

Fat and happy in the backcountry!

Food Preparation Fundamentals

Basically you'll be preparing food in one of 5 ways: boiling, baking, frying, grilling and poaching. Purists will insist that some of these are actually broiling, sauteeing, wrap cooking and roasting, but this is not the Culinary Institute of America, and the fine points can be skipped.

Definitions

boiling: Cooking in a liquid at its boiling point. Remember that the higher the altitude, the lower the temperature at which this occurs. That's the good news, because it takes less time to get the water bubbling. The bad news is that the lower boiling temperature means you have to cook the food longer than at sea level. The following chart indicates the differences:

Altitude	Boiling Point of Water	
	Fahr	Cent
Sea Level	212	100
2,000 ft.	208	98
5,000 ft.	203	95
7,500 ft.	198	92
10,000 ft.	194	90
15,000 ft.	185	85

baking: Cooking in enclosed heat. At home this means using an oven. In the wilderness it means nesting a covered pot in coals. For best results, the pot is *not* set directly on top of the coals, but on a cleared spot in the middle of the ashes of a fire. It is then *surrounded* by the hot coals. Foil-wrapped food placed on or under coals (or both) is also "baked."

frying: Cooking in fat over direct heat. The fat may be any cooking oil —vegetable, corn, peanut, safflower, sesame—or vegetable shortenings like Crisco, Spry, etc. Margarine works too, if you keep it cool and in a tightly lidded container. Butter and olive oil spoil too rapidly to be practical. Bacon drippings are fine for frying, but bacon doesn't last much longer than butter. We travel with a plastic bottle of vegetable oil and several sticks of margarine in a small plastic container.

grilling: Cooking over direct heat on a rack, grill or stick, a.k.a. broiling or barbecueing. Backpacking grills are light-weight and small. Sticks, if used, should be pointed at one end, green so they don't burn, and long, so your hand doesn't cook along with the food. If the stick is big enough, it's called a spit, and if the food on it is rotated while cooking, this is known as roasting, a technique best left to Tudor kings with very large fireplaces.

poaching: Cooking by simmering gently in just enough water to cover. Simmering describes what water does just below the boiling point: rather than bubble actively, it moves only slightly. This point is hard to maintain on an open fire, but happily it doesn't matter. Boiling works fine instead of poaching.

Practical Suggestions

So much for theory. Practice is more rewarding. In getting started you should take the following into account:

measurements: Our motto is "more or less." You won't have measuring spoons or cups and you don't need them. Approximations, guesses and tasting will suffice. In the following recipes, all of which make enough for 2 hungry adults, we try to keep quantities approximate. Where we use measures, they mean the following:

spoonful: A standard camping kit spoon, about soup-spoon size.

cup: A Sierra-type cup, actually about a cup and a quarter by normal measurements. Sierra cups are lightweight, stack easily, and are less likely to burn your lips when drinking hot liquids than ordinary metal cups, because the rim is made of a heat-resistant alloy. They are available at all camping supply stores.

handful: Just that, an average adult handful.

pots: Our small one holds 4 cups, our medium 8 cups, and our large 12 cups.

Sierra cup.

Other Helpful Hints

meal size: Backpack cooking is cooking in miniature, i.e., a little goes a long way. Be prepared to scale down your normal at-home expectations as to how much you need. You don't want leftovers. Most are hard to store without attracting strange visitors. Plan meals with this in mind. If necessary, feed the last spoonful to the fire or the dogs.

utensils: Pots and pans should be reasonably clean. Make sure the handles don't burn. If you have to stir something on the fire, lengthen your stirring spoon by tying on a stick. Garden gloves also work well to keep your hand from toasting.

water: Have enough on hand for both cooking and cleaning up as you go. A dirty mixing pot often is needed for baking a few minutes later. Lids keep dirt and ashes out. Whenever you remove the top, don't set it down in the dirt. Before replacing, check to be sure you won't be adding any unwanted twigs or leaves.

fire: You want coals more than flame. A blaze burns rather than cooks. It also consumes a lot of fuel.

fire area: A fire requires a flat, cleared area, free of brush and clear of any overhanging branches. Don't put it too near your tent, or a slight wind may fill it with smoke. If the fire area is near some natural "chairs" (a big log will do) or "tables" (like a large flat rock), life is easier.

ingredients: Keep them at hand. You don't want to run all over the campsite for garlic or soy sauce.

white or wheat?: We use unbleached white flour in all the recipes, but whole wheat works just as well.

shade: Keep all food in the shade while you're in camp. You may need to move the food stash several times a day, but it's so little trouble—especially if you keep the perishables together—and so sensible it should become part of your daily routine. If you leave for the day, place the perishables somewhere that will keep the sun off.

tent: A veritable kitchen cabinet—use it. If there are several stages to your food preparation and you need to put something aside, store it in the tent beyond the reach of flies, bees and mosquitos. Be sure, however, that you don't burn a hole in the tent floor with a hot pot. Feel the bottom of the pot, place it on a stone or plate if necessary, and keep it away from sleeping bags and ensolite pads. Don't forget to zip the mosquito flap all the way. Also, be careful of smelly spills; a tent reeking of raw fish or dried white sauce is likely to attract unwanted guests, such as ants or bears. If you have a spare poncho, spread that in the tent before storing food inside; if you do spill anything on the tent floor, wash it thoroughly before dark.

covering food: Foods you cook uncovered at home may need to be covered over an open fire to keep out ash and dirt. In such cases, set the lid on loosely and watch that the contents don't burn.

washing up: Make a wash-up area at the very edge of your campsite so as not to attract insects and animals. Carry water to the wash-up site rather than carrying dirty utensils to a lake or stream. Be sure any detergent, even "biodegradable" varieties, goes into the ground. Those bubbles that you see more and more these days, even in the remotest wilderness areas, won't be going away. We usually wash pots with no soap at all: a little hot water and a good scrubber do fine. If you want to use soap, do so sparingly; a few drops are enough.

when to eat what: Two hot meals a day suffice. They can be breakfast and supper, brunch and supper, lunch and supper, breakfast and lunch — whatever feels good. And there's no fixed order to your meals. If you want nothing but desserts for breakfast, enjoy. One day we made and ate a chocolate cake with chocolate icing, a cherry pie and a loaf of sweet sourdough nut bread. The next day roots and grubs looked great. There's no accounting for the suddenness or strangeness of an attack of the munchies, so you might as well not fight it.

invidious comparisons: Whatever you cook in the wilderness won't be the same as what you make at home. The aim is not to duplicate what you can do seated at the controls of a 21st Century kitchen, but to make do with what you've got. The souffle you bake at 9000 feet might fall flat. It might not even warrant the name you give it. But it will be full of eggs and cheese and trout and will taste at least as good as an omelet. So if you're a hotshot chef in the lowlands, don't despair when things turn out differently from what you think is "right." Hopefully, you'll enjoy the cooking as much as the eating.

Fish

Cooking Fish Without a Pan

You've bagged a couple of rainbows and your partner has taken the required snapshot. The fish are fresh and cleaned; a feast is in order. There are many ways to cook fish: frying or poaching in a pan, stewing or baking in a pot, grilling or broiling over an open flame. For starters, let's say you left your frying pan in the car—at the time it seemed too heavy. The pot lids are too small and light to use as substitutes. The fish are biting on everything from hand-tied flies to Zig-Zag papers, and the idea of one more fish stew palls. What to do? The simplest, most "primitive" method is to cut a green, hardwood stick, sharpen one end, and rub some oil on it. Lay the oiled part in the cleaned, open belly of the fish, and poke the point of the stick into the head to secure it. Truss the fish by poking twigs through one side of the belly, over the stick, and through the other side of the belly. Season it to your taste— with salt, pepper, maybe a dash of lemon juice and a few drops of hot sauce—and grill it marshmallow-fashion over red-hot coals. The smaller the fish, the less time it takes: an 8" trout should be ready in about 6-7 minutes. Check the flesh with a fork. If it flakes easily, it's ready to eat.

If you carry a 3-pronged backpacking grill or a light, round, wire-mesh grill, it's even easier. Grease it well and put it about 5" above the coals. Secure it at both ends with rocks. The grill should be very hot before receiving the trout; that way there's less chance the skin will stick to it. Some minced garlic and a dash of soy sauce or lemon juice in the body cavity will make your grilled trout taste like it came out of a Japanese restaruant. After about 5 minutes, smear a little oil on the "sunny" side, then turn the fish. A small spatula is useful for this. Use

One stick, two twigs, a campfire and a fresh trout come close to an angling backpacker's paradise

the "flake test" for doneness. Incidentally, this is a great way to cook fish for breakfast: it's fast, easy and delicious.

What happens if the fish falls off the stick or through the grids of the grill into the fire? Get it out fast—a quick flip with two forks usually does the trick. Then start over. If you were squeamish about ashes in your food, you wouldn't be here anyway, and there's the bonus of having your dinner cooked just a little faster. The worst that could happen is the fish'll be charred beyond recognition. So who needs recognition? Extricate the remains, scrape off the heavier layer of char, pour some hot sauce over what's left, and rename it "charcoal broiled trout."

R.C. Rethmel in his exhaustive book *Backpacking* describes yet another primitive way to cook fish without utensils: baking it on a rock. He says to heat a clean, flat rock in the fire, then pull it to the edge, with the flat face upwards. Lay a greased fish on the rock and bake it there. Then use the rock as a plate, scraping it clean when you're done eating.

One of the best and easiest ways is to wrap fish in aluminum foil and bake them in the coals. We carry enough foil for at least one meal made this way. About 2½ feet can be folded small and tucked inconspicuously in some pouch. It's usable only once. And remember, foil doesn't burn, so pack out the remains with your other non-organic garbage.

You can either wrap the fish individually or fashion a flat "oven-pan" with a "folding lid" all from a single piece of foil, and bake as many fish as you have on hand in one batch. Two hints about your foil "pan": first, crimp the edges up on all sides so the juices won't spill out. Second, keep the "lid" opening toward you and not the fire; that way you can open the foil with a minimum of movement when the baking is done, and won't lose the juices.

There are endless variations to this way of cooking. The simplest is to season the cleaned cavity with whatever you have on hand: salt, pepper, garlic slices, tarragon, lemon juice. A little oil sprinkled on the inside and outside is also in order. Foil-wrap the fish tightly and place either on or under a bed of coals. Or sandwich the package between 2 beds of coals. That may be a bit excessive, but it can't do any harm. Coals have a habit of cooling, so expect the fish to take about 15 minutes to bake. You may need to add fresh coals if the originals lose a lot of their heat along the way. If you get good at it, you can test for doneness by poking a fork through the foil, while the fish are cooking. If the fork slides in and out easily, meeting little resistance, dinner is done. Or you can slide the foil out of the heat, open it, and use the flake test. If the fish is not quite ready, simply close up the foil and slide it carefully back into place, heap with coals and continue to cook for 5 or so minutes.

Variations
- Bake in soy sauce, garlic, ginger and Chinese sesame oil.
- Stuff the fish with finely chopped nuts and prunes soaked for an hour or so in brandy and warm water. Add a dash of sesame oil.
- Lay the fish on a bed of cooked rice, add a mixture of chopped nuts and cut-up dried fruits (apricots, raisins, apples, prunes), salt, curry powder and lemon juice.
- If you find any roe (fish eggs) when cleaning the fish, save them. Put the roe back in the cavity with whatever else strikes your fancy and bake.

Pan-Fried Fish

If you carry a cast-iron frying pan into the mountains, you'll develop very strong calf muscles but you won't get too far. If, however, you bring a lightweight, teflon-coated pan, the slight increment in weight will be repaid many times over in versatility and pleasure. You can't cook a pancake on a stick, and it's hell to fry a fish without a pan.

Pan-fried trout are so easy and satisfying that you may not get beyond them in a week in the mountains. Small lake or stream trout are tender, cook fast and need almost nothing to enhance their flavor. A pan, lightly greased and set on a grill or nestled between rocks about 4-5 inches above a bed of coals, and a string of cleaned, lightly seasoned trout are all you need for a first-rate meal. The oil should be hot before you add the fish. Turn them over after about 4 or 5 minutes (sooner if they're small or the fire is very hot) and cook for another 4 or 5 minutes. Sprinkle generously with lemon juice. That's all, folks.

As soon as the flesh flakes with a fork, it's done. Be careful at this stage; an overcooked fish loses a lot of flavor. When in doubt, take the fish off the fire sooner rather than later. You can always put it back, but you can't reverse a burn-out. All our suggestions for minutes per side are approximate. We don't wear watches in the wilderness. It's better to feel for doneness, following the clock in your head, than to put a stop watch on the food in your pan.

One other precaution: make sure the oil doesn't burn. It starts to smoke and turns black if it gets too hot. At the smoking stage, add more oil to the pan to reduce the temperature. By experimenting with the heat of the fire and the height of the pan above it, you'll soon get the right combination and the fish will cook to perfection.

Variations
- Dip the trout into flour (a heaping spoonful is enough for a 10" fish) which has been seasoned with any combination of pepper, rose-

mary, tarragon, basil or ginger. Fry as above, adding finely chopped nuts to the pan while cooking. Sprinkle with lemon juice at the last minute. This is the wilderness equivalent of the famous French dish, Trout Amandine, which means "trout with almonds." Don't worry if you only have peanuts or cashews. It'll taste just as good, and Escoffier is not likely to pop out from behind a tree to point an accusing finger.

- Use a mixture of flour and cornmeal, a level spoonful of each for a 10" fish, and proceed as above, with or without the nuts. Some old-timers put the flour-corn meal mixture in a bag, drop in the fish, shake, and fry.
- Make a small cup of milk with instant powdered milk and water, dip the fish into the milk and then the flour or flour-cornmeal mixture. Fry as above.
- If you have a spare egg, use it instead of milk. Crack it into a pot lid and beat lightly with a fork. To make it go farther, add a spoonful of water to the egg. Dip the fish into the egg and then into the seasoned flour. (These last 2 methods are roughly equivalent to batter-frying.) It's possible to build up an impressive layer, and for some mysterious reason lots of camping recipes call for more batter than fish. This works best if you have very few fish and the makings of lots of batter.)
- Suppose you run out of flour and cornmeal and still want to coat the fish? Crush a couple of RyKrisp or whatever other crackers you have between a plate and your Sierra cup. Using this coarse meal, proceed with or without egg or milk.
- A piece of stale bread or biscuit can also replace flour or cornmeal. Just make a fine layer of crumbs by rubbing the bread between your hands. Ground up nuts, seeds, left-over rice — almost anything'll do. Use your imagination.

Poaching

We've noticed on backpacking trips that we often crave rib-sticking foods, the kind that even in small quantities make us feel full. This may be a genuine physiological need: to replenish bodies that have worked abnormally hard over 2 or 3 days. Or it may be all in the mind: a need to eat a lot when there isn't a lot to eat. Whatever the cause, the consequence is either to eat everything in one sitting and go home, or devise ways of making hearty, bulky meals with what you've got. We prefer the latter. That's where poaching comes in.

If you want a thick stew, curry, trout in white sauce, souffle, or crepes, you won't want to pick bones and skin out of them. To remove these beforehand, simply poach the fish. This leaves the flesh tender and ready to eat; the rest is disposable. Here's how:

Put enough water in your frying pan to barely cover the fish. Season it with salt and herbs to taste. Place the pan over the fire and let the water come to a slight boil. The fish will curl up. That's all right. There's also no need to turn the fish over. It's done when the skin peels off easily, and the flesh has lost its "transparent" look and comes off the bone at a nod and beckon. This takes about 10 minutes from the time the water begins to boil.

Remove the pan from the heat, the fish from the pan, and then with fork, knife or fingers peel off the skin and flake the flesh from the bones. Ideally, the backbone comes off in one piece, taking most of the skeleton and leaving you with a simple mop-up operation close to the fins. It's simple, but work fast or you'll end up wearing a halo of flies and other airborne participants. When finished, place the fish in the tent until ready to use and burn the skin and bones. If you won't be using the poaching water (see "Fish Stew" and "White Sauce" for possibilities), throw it out far from both your living area and the lake or stream.

A poached fish is a finished product. Seasoned well and not over-cooked, it's as tender as you'll get a trout. But a poached fish is also part of a process that involves other methods of cooking. The following 5 recipes will show you how to combine several methods of preparing fish in order to end up with something definitely more than the sum of its parts.

trout tandouri: This is a curry dish. After you've poached and put aside the fish, boil up a pot of rice. About 2 handfuls will do for 3 or 4 small fish. Cut or chop a mixture of whatever dried fruits and nuts you have: a small dishful will be just right. If you have an onion, chop some of it in too, or scrounge around your freeze-dried dinners for dehy-drated onion. Heat up just enough oil to cover the bottom of your frying pan, toss everything else in, season with curry powder, cayenne pep-per and a little lemon juice. Stir frequently. It's done when it's hot. Guaranteed to warm whatever in you is not. A variation of this is to make a white sauce, season it with curry powder and cayenne, toss in the poached fish and serve over boiled rice with nuts and fruit on the side.

fried rice Chinese-style: Poach, bone and skin your trout, then boil up two handfuls of rice. In the frying pan, brown some chopped garlic in Chinese-style sesame oil, regular oil or a mixture. Add the fish and rice. Season with ginger, dry mustard and black pepper, using soy sauce instead of salt. Stir and fry till very hot, then eat.

hidden lake souffle: A souffle is a concoction made by putting cooked food — in this case, poached trout — into a sauce, pumping it up with air provided by beaten egg whites, and baking. This definition may not satisfy the cognoscenti, and our methods will probably plunge them into a deep culinary depression, but they work, and the results are unspeakably good.

A souffle is a 3-stage affair: poaching the fish, making a white sauce with the poaching liquid, and folding in beaten egg whites before baking. Here are the instructions:

- The number of fish isn't important. If you only have one, that will suffice. Four or five 8'' trout seem right. Poach as directed above.
- Roughly a Sierra cup-and-a-half of sauce is right. Make the sauce thick, using 3 spoonfuls of both flour and shortening or oil. If you run out of stock, use water. As it thickens, add 4-5 thin slices of cheese and seasonings to the sauce, and you'll have the cup-and-a-half.
- Separate the egg yolks from the whites. Have 2 containers ready, large for the whites, small for the yolks. (If you've never done this before, crack the egg in half gently against the whites' container, and hold half the shell in each hand. Most of the white will drool into the container by itself. Help the rest by moving the yolk back and forth between the shell halves.)Don't kill yourself to get all the white. It's OK if a little yolk mixes in.
- Stir a spoonful of cooked sauce into the yolks so they won't hard-boil, then add to the sauce to make it thicker and richer. Finally, mix in the fish. Give it one last stir, then remove the sauce from the heat. Now you're ready for the egg-white caper.
- Beat the whites until they're stiff but not dry. This is easier said than done. Basically you're trying to whip air into them. The bigger the pot and the more you agitate the egg whites, the better your chances of ending up with the right product. The first time we tried this, we had only a couple forks for beaters. It's theoretically possible to get whites stiff this way, but practically impossible. Our great discovery the following year was a spring-loaded ''swizzle-stick,'' like bartenders once used. You can find them in some bar supply stores. They're like half an egg beater, and spin as you push the handle down and release it. They're light, easy to pack and just the ticket for whipping egg whites, adding powdered milk to hot chocolate, brandy to coffee and 100 other mixing tasks. If you can't find one, bring the smallest wire whisk you can buy. One egg will get that

mass of fish and sauce off the ground, but 2 will positively send it soaring.

- Be gentle with the egg whites once they're stiff. You can easily puncture their balloon, and the souffle will end up with a specific gravity close to that of lead. So take extra care when you add the whites to the sauce. Lay the whites on top of the sauce; then scoop sauce up from the bottom of the pot with a spoon, and begin covering the whites tenderly. Bring the sauce to the whites rather than the whites to the sauce. When the whites have been thoroughly "folded" into the sauce, lightly grease your middle-sized pot (even if you have to do some dishwashing and pot juggling to get it free and clean), and pour the souffle mixture in. It should come about 1/3 of the way up the pot, depending on how much fish you have. Cover and bake.

- You've already got a fire going (to poach and thicken the sauce) so by now the coals are glowing red. Scoop out a pot-sized depression in the ashes near the front of the fire and set the pot down—not on the coals, but on the cleared ground or warm ashes. With a heavy stick, pile coals around the pot until it's nestled up to its lid in heat. If the coals are too hot, the souffle will burn. If they're too cool, it'll take ages to cook and you'll do a slow burn with it. Ideally, the coals should have lost their most intense heat; the fiery red glare should be going out of them. Baking time will be about 20-30 minutes, or a chapter from a good book. You may need to add coals to the pile to keep its warmth constant.

- It's permissible to peek but be careful not to knock everything awry or get ashes in the pot. Don't worry if the outside of the souffle is slightly burned; the inside will be as tasty as promised. The souffle *will* actually rise, almost double its bulk, and will look spectacular. However, it deflates rapidly after you take it off the heat. But by then, who cares?

trout crepes: Once you can poach a fish and prepare a sauce, you also have the makings of the filling for crepes. For the filling, poach, skin and bone your fish, add it to a thick sauce made with the poaching liquid, sliced cheese and whatever seasonings you like. Crepes are made with eggs, so you don't need any in the sauce. Keep the sauce warm, near the fire, and covered while you make the crepes (see pp. 159-160). It's neither easy nor necessary to make all the crepes at once, so eat them in turns as they come off the fire. Put a crepe on a plate, spoon sauce into it, wrap and eat. Then let your partner(s) follow suit.

trout, rice and bean salad: Here's an idea for preparing left-over poached trout when you've had an abundance of luck. Just add flaked trout to Bean-Rice Salad (p. 156).

Trout Flambe

Plan to serve this spectacular dish after dark for best effect. Pan fry the fish any style (pp. 145-146). Just before eating, pour a little brandy in a Sierra cup, hold it over the fire until it's warm to your touch and light it with a match. As the brandy catches fire, pour it over the trout. A soft blue flame will dance over and around the trout for up to ½ minute and will add yet another delicate flavor to the dish.

Sashimi (*Japanese-style Raw Fish*)

This book does not aim at conversions. If the idea of eating raw fish turns you green, move on to sauces. But if you like *sashimi,* learn how to prepare it, because you'll never have fresher fish than the ones you catch. Here are some important facts about preparing *sashimi* in the wilderness.

- The fish must be absolutely fresh. They can't sit around for a couple hours in a pot, even cleaned. You need to eat them soon after catching, or keep them alive until you have enough (say, four or five 8'' trout) for a meal. Incidentally, if you're fishing near a snowfield, you can pack your catch in snow immediately, and have them as iced as your local fishmonger's.
- There's not much flesh on a small trout. Some is also lost in skinning and boning. Don't expect a filling meal, but *sashimi* is a perfect lunch snack.
- There are 2 ways to prepare it. In both, clean the fish thoroughly. In the first, skin it and peel the flesh from the bones. To skin a fish, begin by cutting under the fins and yanking them toward the head. Then slice along the backbone from head to tail. With your knife, loosen the skin around the gills. Now work your fingers, the knife, or both, under the skin at the head and strip it back toward the tail. Once the fish is skinned, cut away the flesh, beginning at the backbone and working down. Toward the end, fingers work better than a knife. Place the raw fish in a Sierra cup.
- In the second method, bone the fish first, then remove the skin. Spread open the cleaned and beheaded fish, the gutted side facing you. With your knife cut gently along one side of the backbone from top to tail. Do the same on the other side. This severs the spine from the skeletal bones or ribs, and it can be pulled out, working from

neck to tail. Last, get the skeletal bones out. Starting from the tail, work your blade under the bones gently toward the neck, turn the knife around, and then come back toward the tail. Starting from the neck, lift the bones away. This leaves a whole, flat, boned fish with the skin still on the "under" side. You can now remove the flesh from the skin by working your blade under the flesh and scraping it away. Start at the tail which you can grasp for leverage, and move up. You'll have the fish in one piece this way. Again put it into a Sierra cup.

- One word of caution. All this boning and skinning tends to draw flies. Unless you're fast, you may want to do it in your tent. If so, spread a poncho on the floor so the tent will stay clean even if you're messy.
- You need a spicy condiment with your *sashimi,* as well as some soy sauce. The Japanese use a fiery green horseradish called *wasabi.* This comes in powdered form to which you add enough water to make a paste which is then added to the soy sauce. The fish is dipped into it and eaten straight away. You needn't carry a packet of dried *wasabi.* Dry mustard, particularly the good hot kind, will do just as well and is, frankly, more functional, since you can use it in many other dishes. Either way, *sashimi* is great! Give it a try.

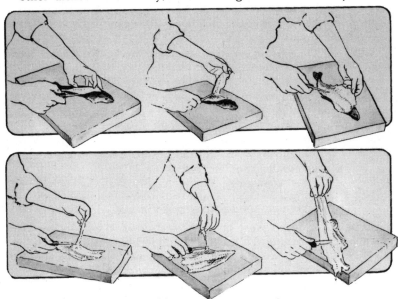

Skinning and boning trout to prepare sashimi

Sauces

You've been in the mountains 8 days and are low on supplies. You have some RyKrisp left, a lump of degenerating cheese, a few spoonfuls of flour, some oil that looks like it came from a crank case and a handful of milk powder. The prospects of catching a trout are dim. You want a hot meal. If you know how to make a sauce, however, you're in business. A combination of oil, flour, milk powder and water will give you a base for the cheese and whatever spices you have left. When it's all melted, thick and steaming hot, you've got yourself a kind of rarebit which can be eaten on the crackers for a filling, hearty meal.

This kind of sauce, practically a meal in itself, can stretch other foods far and in many directions. It has almost as many names as uses: cream sauce, white sauce, bechamel. It's basically equal parts shortening (usually butter) and flour, which are heated for a few minutes before you slowly add liquid (usually milk or the stock with which you've been cooking). That's it. Some seasonings, cheese, perhaps an egg yolk give you sauce thick enough to eat alone or use in a souffle, crepes, curry or cream soup.

At home, you'd use real butter and whole milk. Over an open fire and with neither on hand, the technique changes a bit, but the principle is the same.

In a small pot put 2 or 3 spoonfuls of shortening. Margarine gives you a nicer flavor, shortening the next best, but even oil works fine. For a Sierra cup full of sauce, use 2 spoonfuls to begin with; for more, use 3. Warm slightly, then add an equal amount of flour; for thick sauce the spoonfuls can be slightly heaping. Stir this mixture over the heat for a minute or two to kill the taste of the raw flour. In your kitchen you'd use a low flame. At a camp fire, that isn't so easy; alternate the pan on and off the heat to prevent the sauce from burning. Blend in a heaping spoonful of milk powder and immediately begin adding water, a little at a time, stirring constantly. The mixture will thicken almost instantly. Continue to add water, slowly. By the time you've added a cupful or more, the sauce will have thinned out, much to the relief of anyone who thought they were being conned into making kindergarten paste. Keep stirring until it's smooth. Add lots of seasoning: salt, pepper, dry mustard, cayenne, lemon juice, thyme or paprika. Then perhaps dice some cheese in and melt it. The sauce is done when it's reasonably thick, smooth and tasty. You'll do lots of sampling, but don't eat it all! And don't be alarmed or disappointed if the flour and milk powder aren't completely absorbed by the liquid. It'll still be hot, fil- ling and delicious. When it's done you can add whatever else you want: poached fish, crushed biscuits, cooked rice or noodles.

If the sauce is too thick or pasty, keep adding liquid until you get the consistency you want. If it's too thin, either let the sauce boil down while stirring, or in a pot lid, make 5 or 6 marble-sized balls of dough from flour and shortening or oil. Drop these into the sauce and stir. They'll thicken the sauce without leaving it filled with lumps of unab- sorbed flour which would happen if you added flour alone to the sauce.

Variations
- Instead of using milk powder and water, use the liquid from the poached fish.
- Use both milk powder and poaching liquid.
- Add egg yolks if you're using egg whites for a souffle.
- Add a dash of brandy from the medicine kit.

Rice, Noodles, Beans

You can't always count on catching fish, but you can always count on a hot and filling meal if you have any of these great staples of back- packing. They can be eaten alone, hot or cold (though cooked), in stews and soups, in freeze-dried dinners to add bulk and a little real taste, in puddings, salads, omelets and a thousand other dishes. Their only drawback is that they're heavy, so you need to limit the amounts you take and make do with what you can sensibly carry.

Rice

Put 2 generous handfuls in the medium pot with a pinch of salt. Add enough water to come up to just below the middle knuckle of your fore- finger. This is enough rice for 2 adults. We can't explain the knuckle measure. It was taught to us years ago and for reasons that are still mysterious, is invariably correct. Neither the size of the finger nor the size of the pot seem to matter. Remember: the water will boil faster in the mountains than at sea level. Thus the knuckle measure will give you more water to start off with than you'd use for a good fluffy rice at home.

White rice cooks in about 10 to 15 minutes, depending on the heat of the fire. Brown rice requires more water, to about the middle of the knuckle, and more time to cook. Allow about 25 minutes. To make the pot easier to clean, pour water in it immediately after you've spooned out the rice, and keep it warm near the fire. By wash-up time, the pot almost cleans itself!

Variations
- Fried rice. Chinese or Indian-style with curry (see p. 147). Cook the same way, perhaps adding extra rice to make up for the lack of fish.
- Baked rice in cheese sauce. Make a cheese sauce (p. 152), add cooked rice, and bake or heat until it thickens.
- Baked rice in cheese sauce. Make a cheese sauce, add cooked rice, and bake or heat until it thickens.
- Rice pudding. This can be a meal in itself and is sweet to boot. To cooked rice, add: a spoonful of milk powder, ½ cup of water, 2 or more spoonfuls of sugar, a pinch of salt, some cinnamon, an egg, a dash of lemon juice, ½ spoonful of margarine, some chopped dried fruit and a hit of brandy, which is a nice substitute for vanilla. (Too many ingredients? Not really; check those food lists in Chapter 3. You have all the makings *well within* your weight limit!) Grease a medium pot and line it with crushed RyKrisp or crackers. Add the rice mixture, sprinkle crushed crackers on top, cover and bake in the coals until it's set, about 30-40 minutes. Eat hot or cold.

Suppose you don't have a spare egg? It may not be as rich, but you can still make a pudding. Substitute flour or cornmeal. Likewise with margarine: use oil or shortening. Ditto for the seasonings — not everyone carries lemon juice or even cinnamon (although no backpacker carrying cinnamon has ever been known to starve in the wilderness). You may want to throw in some Swiss Miss powdered chocolate drink instead of sugar and cinnamon. Fine. And of course, the cracker crumbs can be left out. Experiment. Enjoy.

Noodles

You *can* pack gallons of spaghetti sauce into the mountains, but frankly, the water content makes it too heavy. We've tried it. One year we backpacked with a spaghetti junkie who insisted. The sauce was great, but the agony of getting it up was not worth the ecstacy of getting it down. Spaghetti itself has limited uses. Other pastas, like elbow macaroni, egg noodles, Chinese or Japanese noodles are better suited to the mountains. They can be boiled, baked or fried as substitutes for rice in any of our recipes. Cold, they make a salad when mixed with some lemon juice or vinegar and oil, a little dry mustard and some bean sprouts (see p. 164).

Noodles don't double in bulk when cooked, but the more water you use the less they stick together and to the pot. Use the large pot, ½ to 3/4 full of water, add salt, boil, and throw in the noodles. Two very generous handfuls will get 2 of you through a meal. The water should boil rapidly as they cook. They taste done in about 10-12 minutes. If you plan to use them in another dish you need time to put together, just drain the noodles, add fresh cold water to cover and let them stand. .This prevents them from sticking together. When everything is ready, drain them again, and away you go. If you make a sauce, use the noodle water as the liquid base. It's already hot and flavorful.

Remember that noodles are much bulkier than rice. They're also more fragile. Also noodles are used as components in many freeze-dried dinners (beef stroganoff, spaghetti and meat balls, tuna casserole, to name a few) and thus are available in lighter, more convenient form than if you packed them in whole. There's no rule that says you have to eat the components of a freeze-dried meal together. Use the noodle packet in any of our recipes, and finish off the rest of the freeze-dried dinner as your imagination sees fit.

Beans

Beans are so good, nutritious and easily prepared that it's a pity they weigh so much. Nevertheless they are definitely worth taking along, in limited amounts. And it doesn't matter what kinds you bring: red, kidney, white, black beans — they can all be used with equal ease. Put a couple handfuls in a pot, cover with cold water, cover the pot and soak overnight or for 4-5 hours during the day. Empty the old water, cover again with fresh water, add salt, and cook until the beans are tender, 25-40 minutes, depending on the amount and kind of beans and the heat of the fire. That's all there is to it. By the way, as with noodles, the cooking liquid can be used for making sauces.

Variations
- Fried rice and beans (p. 154).
- Baked rice and beans in cheese sauce (p. 154).
- Bean soup (p. 157, "Drinking Your Dinner").
- Refried beans. Cook the beans (save the water), and add to hot oil in the frying pan. Mash the beans with a fork as they are frying, or use the plastic spatula on teflon. If the beans get too dry, add some of the liquid you reserved. Fry slowly, season with pepper, hot sauce, and slice cheese over them. Eat with biscuits and you have a great Tex-Mex meal.

- Ranch Omelet. For the 2 of you, scramble 3 eggs with the refried beans.
- Bean-rice salad. Soak 2 handfuls of beans overnight, cook and cool. Cook and cool 2 handfuls of rice. Mix together with a handful of bean sprouts and, if you have any, poached trout. Season with salt, pepper, lemon juice, sesame oil, mustard. This is a wonderful meal, even without the trout.
- Bean and sprouts salad. Same as above, though without the rice. Use half beans and half mung bean sprouts (see below). Season with salt, pepper and whatever else is handy.
- Bean sprouts. We always bring some dry mung beans to sprout on the trail. They're a great snack, excellent in soups, fried rice, sauces, souffles, salads. The first night, soak a handful in a plastic bag. In the morning, drain the water, close the bag and keep in a dark place. While hiking, we carry them in the smallest nested pot; at camp, they're stored in the backpack. Rinse once or twice a day to keep moist, but not wet. They'll sprout in about 3 days. They don't need to be cooked, but do get moldy fast, so when they're ready, use them. Then begin a new batch.

Drinking Your Dinner:
Soups And Stews

The dry soup mixes that you buy in the local market taste all right, but they're not very filling. If they're going to be your *supper*, you need to jack them up, give them some body and thus a bit of soul. A handful of uncooked rice or noodles, as much cooked rice and beans as you want, a clove of garlic, a slice of onion, vegetables from your freeze-dried dinner or from your home dehydrator (see p. 175), broken crackers, poached fish, cheese—whatever seems to fit your soup mix, will thicken the pot. Starting from scratch is easy too. Here are a couple of examples.

Fish Stew Or Chowder

Clean 2 or 3 fish, but save the heads. Toss fish and heads into the big pot, cover with water and poach. Save the liquid in another pot, remove and burn the bones, heads and skin, then combine the fish and liquid. If necessary, add water. Toss in 2 handfuls of rice (less for more fish), and as much chopped onion and garlic as you can spare. Season with salt, pepper, herbs, even a dash of hot sauce. Boil slowly until the rice is done. The thicker the better, so a packet of dry soup mix, especially leek, helps immeasurably. Ignore the packet's directions, and keep tinkering with the seasonings until it tastes just right.

Variations
- For Chinese-style "hot and sour" soup, add a good dash of vinegar and considerable black pepper.
- For New England chowder, add a spoonful of milk powder just before it comes off the fire.

Black Bean Soup

Soak overnight and cook 2 handfuls of black beans in the big pot. If you've got a packet of chicken or beef soup stock, add that, as much chopped onion as you can spare, some chips off a bacon bar or jerky, lots of garlic, salt, pepper and cayenne. Bring to a boil and let simmer for an hour if you've got the time and the coals are working right. Long cooking gives it more flavor, but even 20 minutes is fine since all the ingredients have already been cooked. Just before serving, add a dash of lemon juice or vinegar and a good hit of brandy. That's it. You'll want seconds, guaranteed. And if you don't have black beans, use what you have and just call it by a different name.

Lentil Or Pea Soups

If you prefer lentils or dried peas to beans and noodles, take them to use as you would for bean soup. Like beans, lentils and peas need 2-3 hours' soaking before cooking.

Pancakes And Crepes

There's something about the cold morning air, a warm fire, a hot griddle and real maple syrup that make pancakes almost a ritual necessity on a backpacking trip. Here's how to make them.

Ready-made pancake mixes are available in supermarkets. Natural ones are available in some health food and whole grain stores. They're adequate; the only problem is you can't unmix them. All you can do with them is make pancakes. If you do use them as a flour supplement or substitute in breads and cakes, you'll end up with something that tastes and looks like a pancake with elephantiasis. The same goes for sauces: you get a warm pancake batter (with cheese), edible but not particularly entertaining. As long as you're taking flour, eggs and milk powder anyway, why not start from scratch?

Pancake batter is made of flour, eggs and milk, to which some shortening and a leavening agent such as baking powder are added. Change the proportions and you get different kinds of pancakes: crepes, for example. There are only a few general rules:

- Always add the liquid ingredients to the dry. This is a conservation principle: if you start with too much liquid, you'll waste a lot of flour thickening the batter. But starting with flour, you can add the liquid gradually until the batter is just right. Water, after all, is expendable.
- You don't need to grease your pan if the batter is made right. The oil or shortening goes in the batter, not in the pan. A thin film of oil won't hurt, but with a decent pan—it doesn't even have to be teflon-coated—it won't be necessary. Crepes need a little oil in the pan, but not much.
- Heat the pan before you pour batter in. Test by splashing a few drops of water into the pan. If they dance, sizzle and evaporate, you're ready to go.
- The first pancake is a test run. If it sticks to the pan or isn't golden brown, the pan isn't "tempered" yet. Scrape it off. The second won't stick. If the first one tastes like a sodden brick, you need more liquid; a runny mess means you need more flour. With a little refining, the rest of the pancakes will be just fine.

Basic Pancakes

At home, the usual proportion for pancakes is roughly 2:2:2—2 cups flour, 2 cups milk and 2 eggs. In the wilderness, the proportions are the same, though the quantity is reduced. A Sierra cup holds around 6 heaping spoonfuls of flour, which makes way too many pancakes for 2 adults. Our recipes make from 1O-12 inflated "silver dollar" pancakes, more than enough for 2. The cakes are thick, light and filling. You could write home about them. Except there isn't a post office within 3-days' walk.

dry ingredients: Place 4 heaping spoonfuls of flour in the small pot. Add a spoonful of milk powder, a dash of salt, a ½ spoonful of sugar and a pinch of baking powder or soda if you have them. These leavening agents are not necessary; they just make the pancakes rise a little. In fact, the higher you go in altitude, the less of any leavening agent you need (as the atmospheric pressure lowers).

wet ingredients: To one egg add 2 spoonfuls of oil and stir this quickly into the flour. To hell with any lumps! Now add about ½ a Sierra cup of water. The batter will be thick; you may need to add a bit more water, just enough to keep it thick but still smooth enough to flow off a spoon, like a thick velvet ribbon. Don't worry about getting a perfectly smooth batter; lumps will disappear in the cooking.

cooking: Drop a large spoonful of batter in the middle of the heated pan. If it looks pitifully small, add a dollup more. The cake is ready to flip (only once) when bubbles begin to form on the surface. Flip and let it cook another few minutes. The second side never takes as long as the first. That's it. Eat! Or, if the first one is good, make 3 or 4 pancakes at one time so that one of you can have a decent breakfast. Then trade places.

Variations
- Use the same proportions, but separate the egg and use only the yolk. After the batter is ready, beat the white until it's stiff but not dry, exactly as you would for a souffle. Fold the beaten white into the batter gently, to preserve as much of the air as possible. Cook as above. The result will be so light that you'll seriously rethink the theory of gravity.
- Chop apricots, apples, banana chips into tiny pieces and add to the batter.
- Add a ½ spoonful of sourdough starter to the dry ingredients and omit the baking powder (see "Sourdough," p. 163).
- Whole wheat or buckwheat flour, a mixture of flour and cornmeal work well and make great pancakes. So does flour with ground up RyKrisp, ginger snaps or vanilla wafers. Just remember that each kind of flour has a different moisture content, so adjust the liquid accordingly.

Crepes

Crepes are French pancakes. They should be paper thin, to wrap other foods in. To achieve the thinness, change the proportions of flour to liquid to eggs. At home, it would be roughly 2:2:4 (2 cups flour, 2 cups milk and 4 eggs). At 9,000 feet, you're unlikely to have that many eggs to spare. So stick with one egg and follow the basic pancake recipe (see p. 158) with the following changes:
- Omit the baking powder or soda. Instead of a spoonful of milk powder, use a ½ spoonful and increase the water to make a thin batter — thin enough to look drinkable, like a homemade smoothie.
- No self-respecting crepe recipe includes oil in the batter. If tradition counts with you, leave it out and spread a thin film of oil on the pan

for each crepe. We, however, are not so self-respecting, and after making sure the Academie Francaise is not meeting in the nearest bog, we throw in a spoonful anyway.
- If you have time to fish before breakfast, set the crepe batter aside, covered, in a cool spot. Crepe batter is happier if it sits a while. When you get back, poach your fish, crank up a sauce, and savor trout crepes.

cooking: Pour 2 or 3 spoons of batter into a sizzling pan. Tilt the pan away from you, then to the side, then toward you so the batter spreads out roughly in a circle as thin as you can get it. The more you practice, the easier it gets and the rounder and thinner the crepes will be. They'll only take a minute or so to cook and are ready to turn when the center looks almost, but not quite, dry. Either work a spatula underneath to turn it, or pick it up in your hand and flip it over. The second side takes less time than the first. The result should be cooked but also pliable, so it can be wrapped around food, and it shouldn't taste doughy.

Variations
- Aside from the fabled trout crepes (p. 149), make cheese crepes (p. 152, sauces) or Burrito Manque (Fake Burritos), using crepes as tortillas to fill with fried beans, rice and sliced cheese.
- Dessert crepes are a delicacy which require a warm sweet fruit filling, made like a jam by simmering cut-up dried fruit and sugar in a little water until it turns into a sweet, thick glop. Stuff the crepes with the fruit, sprinkle sugar and cinnamon on top, and serve. These are also fun to flambe (p. 150) after sunset.

It's all in the wrist

Breads

Anybody who can make pancakes can make pan-fried bread. And anybody who can make the dough for pan-fried breads can add some yeast and bake the bread in a pot in the coals. And anybody who can do that can just as easily make a cake. No excuses.

For pancakes, the liquid ingredients outnumber the dry and you end up with batter. In bread, the opposite is true and you end up with dough. The dough can be picked up without running down your sleeve and dripping all over your shoe. It can be folded or spindled without harm. A cake is somewhere in between: in other words a stiff sweet batter and the promise of dessert. There's considerable lore about campfire breads and cakes, such as bannock, the basic pan bread, so basic it consists of little more than flour and water with a little baking powder and salt tossed in for luck; sourdough, the old-time, home-made substitute for yeast once carried around in pots hung from the saddle in gold country. But lore's a bore when you're hungry. Here are some of our favorite mountain breads.

Pan-fried Breads

This recipe is so uncompromisingly basic that it has little to recommend it except to give you an idea of how simple bread-making is. Try it once for experience, then move on to the tastier variations.

In the medium-sized pot mix together 4 heaping spoonfuls of flour, a 1/4-spoonful of baking powder, and a pinch of salt. Add enough water to make a stiff, smooth dough you can pick up and handle without it sticking to your fingers. Have the flour sack handy so you can keep both hands floured; and if necessary, add small increments of flour to the dough to get the right consistency. Put a layer of oil in the frypan to preheat, and form 6-8 small patties of dough, about the size of a muffin and ½-3/4'' thick. (If you like flipping them in the air, cook one at a time.) Let them brown slowly over a moderate bed of coals. If the fire is too hot, the crust will cook too fast, leaving the insides half raw. Flip or use a spatula to turn them, as often as you like. They're done when they sound hollow to the tap of a finger, roughly 15 minutes, and are more than enough for 2 ravenous adults.

Variations
- Corn-meal muffins. In the medium pot, mix together 2 heaping

spoonfuls of flour and 2 of corn meal. Add a pinch of salt, a spoonful of sugar and one of oil, a ½-spoonful of milk powder, and a 1/4-spoonful of baking powder. Mix thoroughly, then add enough water to make a smooth dough, easy to handle but not sticky. Keeping your hands lightly floured, form the dough into whatever shape suits you. Cook as above. The result is indecently good, a cross between English muffins and old fashioned corn fritters, or something like famous Southern Hush Puppies. Eat plain, with a sprinkling of sugar, or split open and cover with maple syrup. They're also great with grilled or foil-baked fish.

- Vary the proportions of flour to cornmeal. Leave out the milk powder or the sugar. Add chopped onion, dried fruit, or chips from a bacon bar. (In this case, increase the amount of baking powder by half.) Or add a spoonful of sourdough starter to the dry ingredients.
- For part of the cornmeal or flour, substitute a packet of dry instant oatmeal.
- Dust the muffins with cornmeal before you fry them.
- Season with pepper, nutmeg, cinnamon, sesame seeds, or a small amount of crushed nuts.

Baked Breads

Baked breads involve one more step than pan-fried, and a lot more time. The extra step is mixing a leavening agent into the dough to lighten it—to puff it up with a myriad of tiny bubbles, making it rise before it's baked. The mixing must be thorough, so you have to punch and push—or "knead"—the dough fully. There are many leavening agents; yeast is the most famous, sourdough starter is another. We carry several packets of store-bought dry yeast with us, and take along a small plastic bottle with sourdough starter. Baking powder and soda work only under extreme heat (in the act of baking itself) and can't be used for pre-bake rising.

starting the yeast: All leavening agents work by slowly releasing gas, which gets trapped in the dough and which, in trying to get out, forces it to expand. Yeast needs warmth to produce the gas. In the wilderness, the sun is your warmth. It's also possible to use the warmth of dying coals, but the sun is always your best bet. Don't plan to let your bread rise at night.

Yeast is also activated by warm water and sugar; it's inert until this is done. Sometimes it gets too inert or stale: check the date on your yeast packets. It should read at least a couple months ahead. To activate, sprinkle the amount of yeast you need, usually a packet or less, add a ½-cup of water comfortably warm enough to keep your finger in. Add a couple generous pinches of sugar, mix thoroughly, cover and set aside in a warm place until you're ready to add it to the dough. When the yeast is frothy and expanding, it's ready to use.

Starting The Sourdough

Sourdough is exactly that: a dough made of flour and water that has begun fermenting, thus growing microscopic organisms that give off carbon dioxide gas and a characteristic sour smell as they feed. In its working form this is called a "starter" because, like yeast, it initiates the leavening process. Having carried it into the mountains and hung it in a tree to get warm and smelly, you're ready to use it freely in breads, pancakes, etc.

In theory, sourdough starter is a complete substitute for yeast. In frontier days, it was impossible to keep yeast fresh, but sourdough could be replenished every time it was used, thus keeping it alive and ready indefinitely. The best starter comes from the sourdough pot of a friend whose family has kept it, along with great-grandad's Klondike nugget, for 100 years. Or you can buy dried starter in a health food outlet. But if great-grandad took his starter (and nugget) to the grave, and the store is out, here is a basic starter recipe to make at home before beginning your trip.

Heat a cup of milk, add a cup of water and cool to lukewarm. Thoroughly mix one tablespoonful of sugar, a teaspoonful of salt and 2 cups of flour in a large bowl—it's going to expand. Cover the bowl with a towel and leave in a warm place for 4 or 5 days or until it looks and smells frothy. Now add a package of yeast, after starting it as described above. Recover the bowl, and let sit at room temperature for another week. Stir it down each day and don't worry how it smells or looks: the badder the better. Store in a jar in the fridge until you're ready to use it.

Sourdough starter alone was fine for Yukon prospectors, but frankly it takes so long for dough to rise that it often dries out, leaving you with a loaf that looks and feels like a gold brick. We always add yeast to the sourdough starter, hedging our bets. Things move along at a fine pace and the bread tastes better, too.

Basic Mountain Loaf

A loaf of bread will be as big or small as you have flour to spare. Everything else is secondary. If you have nothing but flour, water and yeast, you can make bread. It might not win prizes at the Happy Valley bake-athon, but it will beat dried-out Triscuits. And with a few additional ingredients like salt, milk powder, sugar, oil, sourdough, raisins, nuts, cornmeal, oatmeal, a spare egg, onion, garlic, cinnamon, nutmeg, sesame, poppy or sunflower seeds, to name a few your breads will become a hedonist backpacker's dream-come-true.

The following recipe makes about the smallest loaf that is practical and still plentiful for 2 people. To double it, use twice as much flour, the same amount of yeast, salt and milk. Smaller pots bake better, though a bigger bread will require a larger pot.

Your basic utensils are: 2 pots, a plate, a Sierra cup, a spoon and eventually, a bed of hot coals.

To ½ a Sierra cup of warm water, add a packet of yeast and a couple pinches of sugar. Cover and set in a warm place. In the medium pot mix together: a Sierra cup of flour, a generous dash of salt, one spoonful each of milk powder, sugar, and oil or melted margarine. Mix the bubbly yeast into the pot thoroughly. The result will be lumpish, perhaps soggy. Never mind. If a lot of the flour is still dry, add a bit more water, not much. You want a fairly stiff dough, not a batter.

Now turn this out onto a floured plate or flat, clean floured rock. Flour your hands and keep the bag nearby. The aim is to turn this sodden stuff into smooth, springy, velvety dough. Do this by kneading, that is, by folding the dough over and over on itself. Use the heel of your palm to push the dough away from you, fold it back on itself, give it a 1/4-turn, repeat, turn, repeat, and so on. If the flour on your hands and the plate don't suffice, add flour in very small amounts, and knead thoroughly before adding any more. As you knead, the dough will take shape, becoming firm and springy. Conversely, if it gets too hard to knead (or is hard at the outset), you have too much flour and need a little more liquid, either water or oil, the latter being easier to work in at this stage. Soon, the consistency will be just right. The dough is easy and pleasurable to work. You may find yourself spacing out and kneading just because it feels good. It can't hurt, so enjoy it. No harm if you want to go on for a ½-hour, though 5 or 10 minutes should suffice. The finished dough will spring slowly back when you poke a finger into it. Don't be dismayed if the dough takes on the hue of your pot-blackened hands or picks up small pieces of dirt. You won't taste or see it, nor contract some dread mountain disease.

When the dough is kneaded to perfection, it's ready to rise. Grease or oil the small pot, bottom and sides, and drop in the dough ball. Roll it around so its surface gets fully coated with oil. Now remove the dough, re-oil the pot and dust it with a little flour, a process to help prevent the baked bread from sticking. Set the dough back in, cover, put in a warm place and go off to fish, read, sleep, whatever, for an hour or so while the dough rises to double its original bulk.

What's a warm place? Any sun-exposed spot is ideal, unless the sun is searing; then warmth in the shade will be fine. A tent in the sun works; sometimes we stow the pot in a sleeping bag if the day isn't too warm. Avoid setting the pot near the fire. It may get too hot and bake the bread.

What if it clouds over and gets cold? Not to worry, the rising just takes longer — all day is all right. If it's not ready before bedtime, wait till morning, knead the dough some more to bring the spring back, and let it rise again. It's ready to bake when it's doubled in bulk. Incidentally, if you have time, breads are lighter and tastier if you let them rise twice, punching down the dough after the first rising and allowing it to double again. Literally, make a fist and jab the dough in mid-section. It will deflate. Then cover it and let the rising continue.

It's perfectly kosher to peek at the working dough. But it isn't an elevator; you won't be able to see it rise. If things go right, it will rise even if it takes time. If everything goes wrong and it won't rise, just turn it into a cake (see "Getting a Rise Out of a Dud," p. 167-168).

What if it doesn't rise and you don't want a cake? Pretend it's fully risen and bake anyway. The fire's heat gives a last lift to the dough, so the finished loaf will be fine; somewhat heavy but just as tasty. Let's assume, however, that the dough did double, it didn't rain, the coals are still hot, and you're ready to bake. If you wish, gently spread a light film of oil or melted shortening over the top of the dough with your fingers or the underside of a spoon. The oil will give a beautiful brown color to the top crust.

Oven-baked bread is usually started at a high temperature (400 degrees or higher); then after about 10 minutes the heat is reduced to 350 or 375 degrees to finish the baking, normally about 50 minutes. To reproduce those conditions in a bed of coals isn't easy; though, as anyone who has ever made "coffee can bread" at summer camp knows, it's possible. The basic notion is to nestle the pot in a clearing in the warm ash or dirt, pile hot coals around it, then let them cool as the bread bakes. As more coals are needed to maintain the heat, rake them around the pot. On windy days, when the fire burns hot to windward and cool to leeward, rotate the pot 180 degrees every 15 minutes to assure an even distribution of heat.

Baking time differs according to the heat of the fire (which burns slower with wet, faster with dry, and hotter with soft wood), the size of the loaf and its ingredients. The basic mountain loaf should take be-

Don't forget to use a pot-holder when you rotate your stew on a windy day

tween ½ hour and 45 minutes. It varies; keep checking. If the loaf sounds hollow when you tap it sharply, it's done. Remove the pot from the coals and set it to cool for 10-15 minutes. Under the best circumstances, when nothing has stuck to the sides, the loaf will come out when you turn the pot over and give it a couple of sharp raps on the bottom and top edges. Normally, though, you have to run a knife blade around the edges. In the worst of cases, so much will stick to the sides and bottom that you may have to saw the loaf in half and dig it out in sections. Usually, however, patience, cooling, deft use of the knife and a sharp knock of the pot against a rock brings forth a gorgeous golden loaf. Let it cool, then be prepared to defend your share against alien invaders from outer space—or your partner—intent on scarfing it down in one megabite!

No doubt about it, the Basic Mountain Loaf is a taste of backpacking heaven. Using the rough ratio of a generous cup of flour to an ungenerous half-cup of liquid, a packet of yeast and kneading until you get a smooth, unsticky, springy dough, you can overcome all but the most exotic forms of munchies. But the variations are better, and within each variation are other endless permutations.

Variations
- Sourdough Bread. Use the same proportions and ingredients as above, but add a spoonful of sourdough starter when you add the yeast. Depending on the starter's thickness, you may have to add a little more water or flour to the dough.

- Sourdough Sponge. This is a mixture of ½ the flour and all the water you'll use in the bread plus a spoonful of the sourdough starter. It should be sticky and a bit thicker than batter. Set the sponge aside in a warm place to sour for a couple of hours, then add the remaining flour, salt, oil, bubbling yeast, etc., and proceed as above. If you want to add chopped nuts, do so while kneading.
- Raisin-Nut Loaf. Also known as cinnamon-nut loaf, apricot-nut loaf, banana-nut loaf, mango-nut loaf, prune-nut loaf, nut-nut loaf. This one's sweet. Double the sugar, and add some cinnamon along with a good dash of baking powder or soda — which help enormously when fruit is involved. At the kneading stage, add ½ a handful of mixed raisins or finely chopped dried fruits and nuts. Proceed as above. Before baking, sprinkle the top with cinnamon, sugar and more chopped nuts.
- Jelly Roll Bread. While the bread is rising, boil some dried fruit, sugar and water into a thick jelly. Punch down the dough and pat it out on a floured plate. Spread the jelly mixture on top of the flattened dough, roll it up and plop it back into the greased pot for a second rising. You can do the same sort of thing with a sugar-cinnamon-nut paste, using enough margarine to hold it together, and come up with the backpacking equivalent of a morning Danish.
- Oatmeal Bread. Prepare a packet of instant oatmeal as though you're making breakfast, let it cool while you put together the dry ingredients (omitting the sugar) and start the yeast. Add the oatmeal along with the yeast and mix thoroughly. Continue as above.
- Onion and Garlic Bread. Fry a large spoonful of chopped onion and garlic until they're translucent. Mix them into the dry ingredients of the Basic Mountain Loaf.
- Egg Breads. An egg in any of the above recipes enriches the bread and adds more taste. If you use one, you may need more flour.
- Mountain Challah. When you add the yeast, throw in an egg or 2. Mix thoroughly. You may need more flour than usual to absorb the extra liquid. If possible, let this loaf rise twice. If you have eggs to spare, use a third, separated, as follows: Throw the white into the dough at the outset along with the other ingredients, but save the yolk. Then, just before baking, beat a ½ spoonful of water into the yolk, and brush the top of the loaf with the egg and water mixture. It will produce a burnished golden finish that will drive neighboring backpackers into a near frenzy.

Getting A Rise Out Of A Dud

What happens if the dough doesn't rise? You did everything right.

The yeast bubbled and frothed, the dough kneaded nicely, the sun has been shining for hours. But by mid-afternoon, you have an inert grey mass of dough that looks near death. This happened to us on a recent trip. Our options were to toss it or change it. Rick started to reason, like Marie Antoinette, that if you couldn't give them bread, let them eat cake. What wouldn't rise with yeast might with baking powder and whipped egg white. So we added enough water and milk powder to turn the dough into a batter, threw in some baking powder, and came up with a great nut-and-raisin cake.

Some research gave us clues as to why that particular dough didn't rise. Experts have countless reasons to explain failure. Humidity and air temperature affect yeast. Too much sweetener slows down or stops the process. Too much salt also inhibits rising. And too little white or whole wheat flour makes matters worse. That's because wheat flour contains a magic substance, gluten, which gives dough the necessary elasticity it needs to trap the yeast-produced bubbles of gas, allowing the dough to rise. Corn meal, rye and rice flour, etc., have less or no gluten. The dough is made more porous as these are added, and the gas escapes, leaving you with a mound of play dough.

In our case, the dough had too much maple syrup and cornmeal relative to the amount of white flour. It's hard to give exact proportions, especially as you may run out of important ingredients on the trail. But as a rough rule of thumb, try these:

First, a ½ spoonful of sugar or a full spoonful of honey or syrup is plenty for starting the yeast. If you want a sweeter bread, add the rest of the sugar to the dough, but remember that the sweeter the dough, the longer the rising time.

Second, use at least ½ white or whole wheat flour to all the other dry ingredients. If you're running too low on flour for that ratio, consider making cake instead of yeast bread.

Cornbreads

If you like cornbreads which rise, substitute cornmeal for ½ the flour in the Basic Mountain loaf recipe. Add a healthy hit of baking powder or soda and proceed as above.

If you're low on yeast, use a ratio of 4 spoonfuls cornmeal to 2 of flour and forget the yeast. Add a spoonful of baking powder, a shot of salt, a heaping spoonful of milk powder, 2 or 3 spoonfuls of sugar, a beaten egg or 2 and enough water to make a thick batter, similar in consistency to a thick pancake batter. Turn this into a well-greased pot. Bake at once, for ½-3/4 hour. Since cornbread won't sound hollow to the tap, you'll know it's done when the top splits open a bit, and when a knife blade inserted in the middle comes out clean.

Pizza

Ranger Ron said it couldn't be done west of Chicago. It's all very well, he argued, to bake bread in a pot, but pizza has to be flat, and the oven has to be hotter than you can get in the wilderness. We showed him something. Pizza is just an open-baked hot bread with lots of good things piled on top. If you have a frying pan with a removable handle, or a pie plate and a piece of aluminum foil, you can bake a gorgeous pizza in the wilderness.

First, use the Basic Loaf recipe to make dough. Omit the milk powder and sugar. If the dough is too dry after adding the yeast mixture, add a little more oil, up to another spoonful, before using more water. If it's moister than average, don't worry. Knead and set it aside to rise.

When the dough is doubled in bulk, chop or cut up any or all of the following: poached trout, cheese, salami, dried mushrooms, garlic, onion, bean sprouts, dried zucchini. You're unlikely to have tomato sauce, unless there's some in a freeze-dried dinner packet. But you don't really need it to make a pizza, despite what Ranger Ron's Windy City granny will tell you.

To assemble, spread a thin film of oil over the frying pan, including its sides. Punch the dough on a plate and with your fingers work it into a thin, flat circle. You can even pick it up and toss it into the air with a

Campfire pizza

spiral motion, like they do at Momma Mia's. It's helpful to catch it. You may need a little flour on your hands for all this. When the pizza dough has become a nice, even circle, fit it into the pan. It should extend part or all the way up the sides. Then pile on the goodies: tomato sauce first if you have it, then fish, cheese, vegies, etc. Season with salt, pepper, oregano, thyme, basil, whatever tastes Italian. Drip a very thin layer of oil over the finished product, and cover the pan with foil.

Ron was right in one respect. The idea is to bake the dough fast, before you burn everything on top. Pizza ovens are extremely hot (about 500 degrees F). But if you put your frying pan or tin plate on a bed of very hot coals, you'll end up with something you might have to call cheese-n-charcoal. Instead place the pan on cleared ground, surround it with hot coals, and slide coals on top of the foil. Let it bake for 10-15 minutes. Then work some moderately warm coals under the pan and push others around it and on top. In another 10-15 minutes the pizza is done. The dough will be crusty, the cheese melted, and your mouth watering.

Cakes

Making cake on a backpacking trip is sort of like sex on Wednesday afternoon: gratuitous but a lot of fun. It has nothing to do with survival, nor your ability to read a compass, has not one ounce of redeeming moral, social or nutritional value. But as long as you have semi-sweet baking chocolate with you anyway (also great for eating plain because it's unlikely to melt in your pack), some margarine, sugar, eggs, flour, baking powder and powdered milk; and as long as you have the munchies and it's Wednesday afternoon and the sun is high and so's your partner, you might as well hunker down, bake a cake, make an icing, slap the two together, lay back and pig out. It really is a piece of cake.

Basic Cake

Pancakes are the result of frying batter. Cakes are the result of baking batter — batter which contains more sugar and eggs. For an unadorned, ground-level cake, mix together in the medium pot a heaping cup of flour, a big spoonful of milk powder, a ½-spoonful of baking powder and a hit of salt. In the medium pot's lid, cream together a big spoonful of margarine and 3 spoonfuls of sugar. The underside of a spoon is perfect for this. Oil will work, but margarine is better. When the sugar is thoroughly worked in, break an egg into the mixture and beat until the glop is smooth. Add a shot of brandy as a substitute for vanilla. Now combine both mixtures with enough extra water to make a smooth, thick batter that will pour like a ribbon into a well-greased small baking pot.

You'll bake the cake in coals that are cooler than for bread. At home, you'd use a moderate temperature, 350-375 degrees. Out here, start with coals beginning to turn black and try to keep any you add roughly the same color. If you can't, don't worry. Betty Crocker won't be around, peeking over your shoulder. Baking time will vary, as usual, but should run about ½-3/4 of an hour. Test for doneness by inserting a knife blade into the center of the cake. If it comes out clean, the cake is probably done. Remove it from the pot; if you find the middle isn't quite done, put it back in the pot and into the coals for a while, then test again. Once it's done, cool it, and eat or ice (p. 172).

Variations
- Man Eatin' Basic Cake. Follow the recipe above, only separate the egg, reserve the white, and add the yolk to the sugar and butter mixture. When the batter is ready to pour into the baking pot, gently fold in the egg whites, beaten stiff but not dry. This makes the cake even lighter, a cruel blow to weight watchers and lifters alike.
- Advanced Man Eatin' Cake. For a moister, richer cake, use 2 eggs, separate both and proceed as above. Add other things to the batter: cinnamon, Kahlua in addition to or instead of the brandy, several squares of chocolate shaved with a knife, or assorted dried fruits and nuts.
- Chocolate Cake. Set up as for Man Eatin' Basic Cake, reserving the egg whites. Boil some water in a pot. Remove the wire handles of a smaller pot lid and float the lid on the heated water: you've just made a backpacker's double boiler. Place a square of semi-sweet baking chocolate, or a row of German Sweet chocolate, or a combination of both in the lid. As the chocolate melts, add a 1/4-cup of water and stir. Remove from heat and let it cool a bit. Add it to the egg and sugar mixture along with a little brandy. Proceed as above, folding in the egg whites last.
- Surprise-delight Cake. Suppose you don't have all the ingredients and still want to make a chocolate cake. Use what you have. Substitute carob for chocolate; scrape carob off a Tiger's Milk Bar to melt in water. Or melt the whole bar and add it to the egg and sugar mixture. Or use powdered Swiss Miss. If you don't have anything to beat the egg whites with, leave them whole. No baking powder? Use beaten egg whites as a rising agent. No brandy? Forget it. No sugar?

Double the amount of chocolate, or use both chocolate and instant cocoa, which has plenty of sugar in it. Stretch your mind. Just keep the proportions of wet and dry about the same so the batter stays the proper consistency.

Chocolate Icing

All you need here is chocolate and shortening. In the medium lid melt 2 squares of semi-sweet baking chocolate or 3 rows of German Sweet chocolate in about 1/4 cup water stirring as it melts. If you have milk powder, put about ½ a spoonful in the melted chocolate. Now add a spoonful of margarine or shortening and stir until that melts, too. Over the fire, continue stirring until it begins to thicken—chocolate does this as it's heated. Then set it aside to cool. If you have some brandy, add it to the icing now. As the icing cools, it will continue to thicken as the melted shortening rehardens. To hasten this, especially on a hot day, set the lid in a larger lid filled with cold water. Never mind if it doesn't thicken as much as you expect. Just spread it on the cake with a spoon or knife. The result is so good you'll have difficulty waiting for your partner to return from a day hike.

Fruit Cake

This is a mixture of fruits and nuts held together with a mixture of eggs, sugar and flour. It's a snap to make and a great way to use up nuts and fruit before packing out. In a medium or large pot lid, put as much cut up fruit and nuts as you wish. For the smallest fruit cake, about 3 large handfuls will do. To this add a beaten egg, 3 spoonfuls of sugar and a hit of brandy. Mix thoroughly. Now add a dash of salt, a

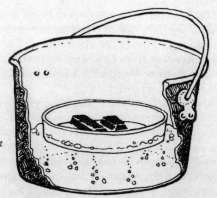

Backcountry double-boiler is perfect for icing on the cake

spoonful of baking powder and enough flour (about 3 spoonfuls) to hold the mixture together. Pour into a well-greased small pot, cover and bake very slowly in moderately hot coals. At home, you'd bake at only 300 degrees, so these coals will be the coolest you've used. Allow an hour or so to cook, and don't expect it to rise much. You'll know when it's done by looking at the top—which should be brown—and testing with a knife for firmness. Run the knife around the edge, turn the pot over and bang it sharply on a rock to get the cake out. If it won't come out whole, cut it in pieces or eat it right from the pot. When the cake is cool, pour some brandy over it and let it sit for as long as you like. It'll keep for days. Incidentally, if it comes out of the pot whole, the cake will be very beautiful.

Cookies

The hardest part of mountain cookie baking is deciding on the ingredients. Chocolate chip, cinnamon-nut, oatmeal, lemon only begin the possibilities. The ratio of ingredients should be 4 flour (including oatmeal) to 2 sugar to 1 margarine. Begin by "creaming" ½ a Sierra cup of sugar and 2 spoonfuls of margarine into a paste. Add an egg and a splash of brandy. To a Sierra cup of flour (or flour/oatmeal) add ½ a spoonful of baking powder, a pinch of salt, and a spoonful of powdered milk. Combine this with the butter and egg mixture. Then add your special ingredients—shredded chocolate bars, raisins, coconut, chopped nuts, dried fruit, cinnamon, nutmeg, ginger, etc. Add flour or water as necessary to get the right consistency, half-way between pancake batter and bread dough. The finished mixture should be thick and chunky. Taste it for sweetness. If it doesn't taste really sweet, your cookies will be more like biscuits.

Cookies are baked in a greased pan exactly like pizza (see p. 169). If you have a plate or lid that fits over your frying pan, you can use it instead of foil to hold the top coals. A few coals below will keep the bottom of the pan warm. You can only bake 3 or 4 at a time, so filling the cookie jar is an all-day project. In a pinch, you can make them like pan-fried bread. They may burn a bit on the top or bottom, but if you dip them in coffee or hot chocolate, you'll hardly notice.

Quiche

One of the best things about the kind of improvisational cooking we've been discussing is that you're never quite sure what's going to happen next. For more than 5 years we'd been baking breads, inventing variations of chocolate cake, igniting brandy and generally congratulating ourselves on the smooth workings of our unbridled imaginations. But we'd never made a pie. Too much trouble, we argued. Too hard. Anyway, what would we fill it with? The answer came from Polly, a doctor who'd lived in the Andes, floated down the Amazon, and survived 20 years in the jungle of Chicago. Five days into the high Sierras in the midst of a hail storm and high winds, she announced she'd make supper that night for 6: a quiche. A quiche is a pie, similar to custard pie but with vegetables and cheese as the main ingredients. We wished her luck and set her up in the tent to get out of the wind (it's not easy to work with flour in a gale). Every so often we'd hear a muffled cry for spices, powdered milk or water and we finally put the entire food pack into the tent so she could work in peace. By sundown, the storm had blown itself out and we were all sitting around the campfire complimenting the chef on her work of art.

The first thing to do is to make a pie crust of pastry dough, which is different from bread dough. It consists of a mix of flour and shortening, with just enough water to hold the 2 together. Here's what you'll need to make a crust in an 8'' fry pan: a large pot, spoon, water, 5 heaping spoonfuls of flour, a dash of salt, and 4 spoonfuls of margarine or shortening. Mix the flour and salt together. Add the margarine, and knead until the dough has the texture of cornmeal. Don't worry if there are some pea-sized globules. Now add 2 or 3 spoonfuls of cold water to the mixture, one at a time, blending it in with the spoon or 2 forks. Only add enough water to hold the dough loosely together. One way to tell if it's right is to form the dough into a lightly packed ball. If it falls apart, you need more water. If it doesn't, set the ball on an ungreased fry pan or pie plate, and press the dough with the heel of your hand, working it to cover the bottom and sides of the pan. It should be very thin, not more than 1/8'' thick. But don't worry if it's thicker. It will bake well and taste great.

If you were backpacking in France you might feel obliged to follow the national custom and partially bake the pie crust next. But you're not in France, so skip it. Just go ahead and fill the uncooked crust with quiche goodies: eggs, milk, cheese, bacon, and as many diced dried vegies as you have. (If there's time, let dried vegetable like mushrooms, green peppers, celery or zucchini soak or cook until they soft. But it's not essential; they'll soften in the baking.) You can add a spoonful of flour at this point if you like to help thicken the pot. In a pot, mix together a cup of milk (made with 3 spoonfuls of milk powder and water), 2 beaten eggs (one will do), salt, pepper and a dash of nutmeg, pour the egg, milk and vegie mixture into the pie shell. Sprinkle on as much finely shredded cheese as you can spare. Any cheese will do. The quiche is ready to bake.

If you have another pie pan or tin plate of the right size, invert it to cover the quiche. If not, cover it with aluminum foil like a pizza, and bake exactly as in the pizza recipe. Set hot coals around and on top. After about 20 minutes, when it's half-done, work some moderately hot coals underneath. The quiche is done when the filling is firm and slightly browned. The reason it takes up to 40 mintues to bake is that the pan is shallow, making the transfer of heat a slower process. You'll be ravenous by the time it's ready, so you'll eat it hot. But it's possible to eat quiche cold, too.

Dried Foods

Prunes, let's face it, aren't pretty. And dried apricots have as much resemblance to the item that hangs on a tree as a fast-food hamburger does to a cow. Beef jerky has all the charm and much of the taste of a leather strap. But they all make up in convenience and lightness what they lack in elegance. Store-bought dried foods share another characteristic. They are, almost without exception, expensive. You pay for the convenience of someone else removing the water.

In recent years, the appearance of relatively cheap and efficient home dehydrators has made it increasingly possible to produce your own dried foods. The results are not package-perfect, but they're tasty, nutritious and a whole lot cheaper. Our model, affectionately called El Cheapo, is a round, 4-tray plastic affair that blows hot air through the sliced foods until they resemble a desert fantasy. It works, that's all we ask, and we've successfully dried apricots, peaches, nectarines, plums, pears, apples, bananas, melon, mango, papaya, zucchini, mushrooms, onions, potatoes, tofu. We've made beef jerky which tastes better than the preservative-laden kind in the markets. We've also dried turkey, lamb and veal strips, to name a few unusual trailside snacks. If you'd like to do your own drying, here are some hints:

- Get a good book about home drying. It will make the job easier and surer. (See ''Appendix'' for references.)
- Dry foods as close to the date of your trip as possible. This is particularly important for meat and poultry. Most home dehydrators won't extract as much water as the pros remove, so deterioration occurs faster. We've successfully dried fruit and vegetables as early as 2

months before the trip. But a month can be enough time for the turkey jerky to begin molding, so we try to finish the meats only a few days before we head out.
- Sweet fruits need not be completely ripe before drying. Conversely, sour ripe fruits take longer to dry and turn into sour dried fruits. Taste as you go.
- Reconstitute vegetables and fruits for use in meals by soaking or heating them in water until they soften. Jerkeys don't reconstitute easily, but a long soaking makes them pliable enough for use in meat dishes.

Snow Cones

Whenever you're above 7,000 feet, you're likely to come on a snowfield or remaining patches of last winter's snow hidden from the mid-summer sun. If you're hiking, pull over and make snow cones—they're so refreshing it's like finding a soda fountain along the trail. Fill your Sierra cup halfway with snow and add any or all of the following: instant chocolate, cinnamon and sugar, lemon or lime juice and sugar, Kahlua, brandy, nutmeg, ginger, etc. Eat with a spoon. They're the *real* treasure of the Sierra, madre!

Cooking In The Rain

Several years ago we were settled into a campsite when it began to rain. Forty-eight hours later it was still raining. Then it began to snow. While our sleeping bags got soggy, our spirits didn't even dampen. We kept warm and full. When it's raining or cold outside, we like to keep our insides full of hot foods.

You can't make elaborate meals in the rain. Baking is out—you can't keep wet coals hot. Frying is possible, but unless your fire is protected from the rain or you fry fast, the food gets wet on top while it cooks on the bottom. Also, if the pan fills with water, you'd be poaching, which *is* a practical method. Another is grilling (a rack will not fill with water). A third choice is cooking in a covered pot, which is our usual choice. Soups and stews are great: hot, easy, filling, and need little tending, so you can stay dry under a tree or tarp as they cook. You're likely to catch fish in the rain, and it's simple to grill them quickly or poach them and add to your pot.

Keep the stored food and matches in waterproof containers inside covered packs. When the sun comes out again, dry any damp food or packets to prevent spoilage. And don't go without at least one hot meal a day in the rain. Even a steaming cup of cocoa and some biscuits, or a bowl of oatmeal will keep the spirits up.

Cooking With A Stove

What if you can't build a fire or don't want to? Some places don't permit fires; others require fire permits; still others allow fires when it's not too dry, but cancel permission when your trout flambe might ignite 3 counties into the bargain. Many people object philosophically to burning dead wood or stripping the ground of it. Often there *is* no wood. Sometimes you're too tired to gather it, it's too long a hike to find any, or it's too wet to burn. On these occasions, a compact, ready-firing backpack stove is as desirable as it is necessary.

Cooking with a stove requires a change in tempo. You have to do it fast to conserve fuel. Unless you *like* hauling dead weight, you won't want to carry too many butane tanklets or cans of Blazo into the mountains. Fast is better, and so is simple. Some things you can't do on a tiny one-burner stove. Baked breads and cakes are out, as are foil-wrapped and grilled foods. Quick-fried food is definitely in, but keep in mind that the circumference of heat is smaller than at home or over an open fire: that large pan of frying fish will stay cooler on the edges than in the middle. Still, pancakes, crepes and pan-fried breads cook reasonably fast. Things you add to boiling water are the easiest and fastest of all. Stews and soups, rice and beans, sauces, cereals, puddings, hot drinks are perfect for a one-burner. So are freeze-dried and dehydrated foods.

To give you an idea of what you can and cannot make on a backpacking stove, here is a reference list to the above recipes. The times are based on a Bleuet S 200 butane stove.

- Cooking Fish without a Pan. Not possible.
- Pan Fried Fish. Works fine on the stove. Small fish are more convenient. Save time by boning and skinning big fish. They'll cook much faster.
- Poaching. Excellent for stove cooking. But preparations requiring more than one step might be an extravagant use of fuel. Souffles are out. But you can make the poached fish and sauce, then put the trout in white sauce inside of crepes. How long would all that take? The last time we brought a watch, poaching 2 small fish took about 10 minutes, the sauce 8, and 8 crepes 20 minutes. That's a lot of fuel.

But it could be your one big blowout in a rocky, 11,000 foot basin.
- Sashimi. No problem.
- Sauce. Takes 8-10 minutes at sea level, longer higher.
- Rice, Noodles, Beans. These work fine if you keep the dishes simple. Rice cooks in 15 minutes.
- Drinking your Dinner. Ignore the suggestion for long, slow simmering. Boiling time for ½ a small pot of water is 5-10 minutes. A few more minutes and soup's on.
- Pancakes and crepes. Keep them small, and the one-burner stove works fine.
- Breads and Cakes. Only pan-fried breads which cook very fast. If you make them muffin sized and cook 4 or 5 at a time, you'll have a meal in about 15 minutes.

stove safety: Use it in a sheltered spot, out of the wind and rain. While it's done in an occasional emergency, it's unsafe to cook inside a tent, even in the rain. Fuel can spill, fumes can make you sick, tents can burn. Use your ingenuity to cook outside instead.

Eating On The Trail

When we're camped, deeply immersed in cooking, 2 meals a day are adequate. Hiking, our eating patterns change. A light, fast, early breakfast gives us a fresh start and enough energy to make that long haul to the pass without cardiac arrest from undigested pancakes in the gut. Eating on the trail is part of a pattern of rest and recovery, necessary to put strength back in the muscles and energy back in the system.

Some backpackers eat continually while hiking. They carry a pouch of gorp, and munch away throughout the day on their mixted dried fruits, nuts, candy, coconut, or whatever. Others prefer to snack at rest stops and have a more substantial lunch at a point where tired muscles, sore feet and spectacular scenery call for a longer break. It's amazing how a good meal makes the body willing to go on, and able to do so.

Keep trail food easily accessible. Why empty your pack every time you want a raisin cookie or a Tiger's Milk Bar? And it should be nourishing. Be sure you have on hand dried fruit, chocolate, cookies, crackers, etc. for energy, as well as salami, nuts, jerky, etc. for strength (protein for muscle restoration) to keep you fit. You also need to replace liquid frequently. Be sure you have enough water to drink often, though not necessarily in great quantity. If you're sure of water sources along the trail, you needn't carry much. Water is heavy. But if you're doubtful, keep your canteen full.

Our style includes frequent stops. Often we're more thirsty than hungry, but we also make sure to get some quick energy by sharing something sweet. We lunch at the top of a pass if the weather is as good as the view. We make cheese and salami sandwiches on RyKrisp, eat nuts and dried fruits, a few bean sprouts and plenty of water. If there's a snowfield nearby, we make snow cones for dessert. Otherwise, it's raisin cookies or the last part of yesterday's cake. We take our time; this is a rest stop. Then we set off toward our destination, often cross-country. We try to arrive by mid-afternoon, but not at the expense of as many rest and snack stops as necessary to keep our spirits up and our legs moving. If we need to make camp before our destination, we give ourselves a simple but hot supper. Freeze-dried dinners and a back-packing stove are handy at such times.

Some backpackers have a saying about emergency situations, "When in doubt, sit it out." We have no objections to that, but we've added a few words of our own. When we come to a crossroads, a roaring creek or a mountain pass, our saying is "When in doubt, the food comes out." Friends say that ours are the only camping trips they've ever heard of on which the backpackers invariably *gain* weight. Right. What better vacation could you have, staying full of great food and drink, and coming home rock hard from all the hiking, climbing and packing? Those visions of sugar plums and all the other delicacies will embellish every tale you tell, all winter long. Give it a try. You'll love it.

CHAPTER VIII:
Star Gazing

Basic Sky

Being in the backcountry changes your nightlife dramatically. You're a million light years from Main Street, and the entertainment section, even if you could read it in the failing light, wouldn't do any good. Dinner has been cleaned up and the evening fishing is over; the wind dies down and the clouds disappear. A chill slides into the air. Time for parkas and wool hats, a fire, maybe a ghost story or the wail of a harmonica. You can try to read until the flashlight begins to flicker; you can follow Ben Franklin's "early to bed" advice; you can stroll down by the lake and watch the moon rise. It's never too late for another cup of hot chocolate and brandy. But in the end, eyes invariably drift upwards toward the Great White Way—the stars in the nighttime sky.

You start to look for the Big Dipper, maybe Scorpio or the Pleaides. Though this is where most non-stargazers' knowledge of the sky ends, we've found that almost everyone has a natural curiosity about the stars and their groupings. If you've packed in a star chart, you'll almost certainly reach for it and try to distinguish Cygnus, the giant swan, from Draco, the great dragon. If you don't have a chart, or have never studied the nighttime sky, this chapter will introduce you to one of the greatest pleasures of long summer nights, that of stargazing.

It's an exciting, challenging process to identify planets and constellations. It takes concentration and some patience; like anything else, the more often you try, the more easy and familiar it gets. At first, however, you're lying on your back, staring into a giant half-dome, but the star map is flat, distorting the sky in order to get it down on paper. Also, the sky moves as the earth rotates, so what you see at 7 pm will not be the same as what you see at 2 or 3 in the morning. The stars also change with the seasons; the June sky is not the same as September's. Trees and clouds can block your view; mountains get in the way. A bright moon obscures many stars in its part of the sky. Nonetheless, with a little time and effort, you can slowly find planets, sort out constellations, even identify individual stars. And while you're at it, you're bound to see flashes of shooting stars, blinking satellites, high-flying aircraft, and, depending how far north you are, maybe even a glimpse of the famous aurora borealis—the northern lights.

Star charts throw half the sky at you at once, far too many stars to see or sort out. In this chapter, we show one small section of the sky at a time. We describe each with pictures, instructions and stories. But before you begin, it's good to know a little basic astronomy.

Astronomy 101

Everything—the moon, Earth and planets, the sun and stars—is moving in space. Astronomical distances are so great, however, that aside from shooting stars, nothing seems to move very fast or very much. Most of the motion you observe during the night (or day) is the result of Earth turning. If you picture a spinning ball inside a stationary, star-speckled globe, you'll begin to get the picture. But from a observational viewpoint, it appears as if all the heavenly bodies do move across the sky. So for expedience sake, we'll refer to the sun,

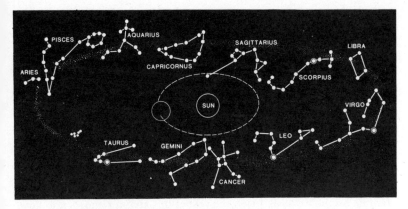

moon and constellations as the moving entities.

Only the star that happens to sit above the North Pole appears not to move as Earth turns; all the rest do appear to move. During the daytime, the sun moves across the midsection of the sky from east to west. During the night, the moon follows a similar path in the same direction. Trace the same arc that the sun and moon describe across the sky and look for very bright stars: the brightest are probably planets. The sun, moon and planets are close to being on the same plane, which paints a wide stripe inside our star-studded globe. They spin and move in circles, but they travel across the sky within that stripe.

Divide that stripe into 12 pieces and you have the 12 "houses" of the Zodiac. Each house refers to a specific group of stars, or a constellation. Ancient astronomers used these 12 houses to keep track of the seasonal and relative positions of the sun, moon and planets, which appear to be stationed "in front" of any given house at any time of month or year. The naked eye may trick you into thinking that the sun, moon and planets are traveling in a high arc "overhead" while the Zodiac is on the horizon, but they are all in that wide stripe running round the equator, just about in the same plane.

It takes the stars in a constellation many millions of years to move in relation to one another. To us, it appears as if they never change position (even though the constellation itself appears to move during the night, due to the spinning of Earth). The sun, moon and planets do move very slowly against the backdrop of the Zodiac constellations. It takes the sun a year to travel slowly through the 12 houses of the Zodiac; it remains in each Zodiac house for a month. The moon travels the same path every month, and is in each house for 3 or 4 days, though even this short passage of time across the constellations is too slow for our eyes to see. On any night, the moon seems locked into its Zodiacal house. However fast it seems to rise and set, it never seems to leave "home." What's happening is that the whole nighttime sky, with the moon in front of a Zodiac constellation, is moving overhead during the night. Saying that the moon is in Virgo means the moon is in that section of the sky occupied by the constellation Virgo. If the sun is in Scorpio, then Scorpio is behind the sun during the day. During an eclipse of the sun, the stars of Scorpio would be visible in that section of the sky.

Of course you don't *need* to know any of this to enjoy the night sky. If you couldn't care less that the Mars Bar overhead is really the Milky Way, then make up your own constellations; rewrite the sky! (See p. 197 for proof it can be done.) If, on the other hand, you'd like to get a handle on the "classic" sky, the rest of this chapter shows you how.

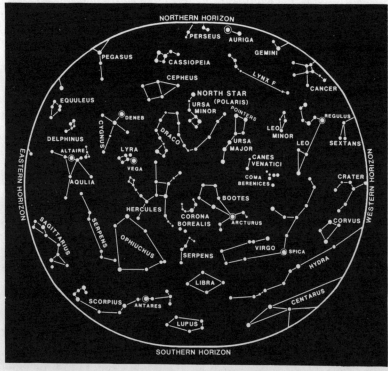

Constellations of summer (9:00 pm). Face north. Hold open book overhead, with top of page toward north

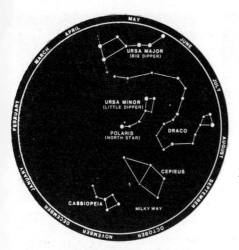

North circumpolar constellations

We'll tell you where the constellations are, what they look like, and how to find them.

Go slow at first. The constellations won't go away. If you find one star group a night, you'll be doing well, and the odds are strong that you'll never forget where it is. Tomorrow night it may be in a slightly different place, but not by much. With a little practice, you'll spot it in September as easily as in July, at 11 o'clock as well as at 9.

We start you off with the major constellations—the easy, circumpolar ones, which revolve in a tight ring around the North Star. Then we proceed to describe the smaller, more distant, and more difficult or obscure ones. At the end we suggest some further reading on both the constellations and general astronomy.

We use a couple of arbitrary devices to help clarify directions and relationships among the constellations: 1) Compass directions (east, southwest, etc.) refer to the earthly horizon. Thus if you're lying on your back looking at the North Star and we send you southwest toward a constellation, trace the direction as you would on a compass: toward southwest on the ground. This may sound obvious, but it isn't when you realize that *all* stars are located literally south of the North Star. 2) We assume, in our directions, that you're facing the sky, holding your star map above—looking *up* at it—and that it's oriented correctly toward the earthly horizon. 3) We show the sky at a theoretical 9:OO pm. To figure out where things are earlier, turn your star map clockwise; later, turn it counterclockwise. A good star map or chart will allow you to adjust for the month: our theoretical June should not upset your own calculations, whatever the time of year.

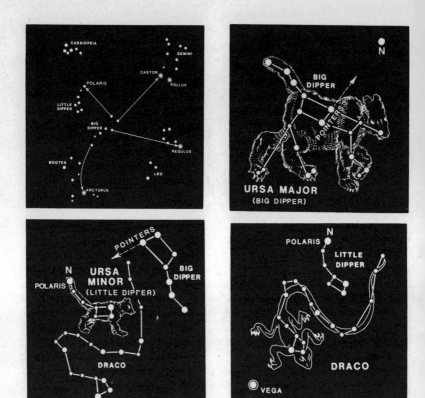

Big Dipper, Little Dipper, Draco

Almost everyone can locate the Big Dipper: 7 bright stars, visible even in the city, a clear constellation in winter as well as summer. Draw a line through the two stars on the end of the Big Dipper's bowl; follow that line three times their distance to reach Polaris, the North Star. During the night, all the other stars in the sky will seem to move; the North Star will remain in place. You can check that you have the right star with your compass, as long as you realize that magnetic north, toward which your compass needle points, is not quite the same as true north, where Polaris sits.

The Big Dipper is actually the hind quarters and tail of Ursa Major, the Big Bear. If you look closely, you can find the bear's paws and outline, but it's not easy. Housatonic Indians saw the four bowl stars as a bear and the 3 handle stars as a hunter with 2 dogs in pursuit. The middle handle star is really a double star; the hunter carried a pot in which to cook the bear. The hunter chased the bear from spring until autumn; when the animal was wounded in the fall, its blood was visible in the leaves of the forest.

For centuries the Big Dipper has guided people to the North Star, which, seemingly "fixed" in the sky, has in turn guided mariners and land navigators in their travels. The North Star acts as the tip of the handle of the 7-star Little Dipper, also known as Ursa Minor. The Persians saw the Little Dipper as a Date Palm; it was a Jackal in Egypt; ancient Norsemen called it the Hill of Heaven, abode of the guardian of the rainbow bridge connecting heaven and earth. It certainly doesn't look much like a small bear.

Beginning between the North Star and the two "pointer" stars of the Big Dipper is a long winding string of stars that goes southeast around the Little Dipper, then back northwest, encircling the Little Dipper on 3 sides. Then it goes southwest again, ending in a rectangle of 4 stars. This is Draco, the Dragon. The Hindus called it an Alligator and the Egyptians, a Crocodile. To the Greeks, it was the Monster Serpent killed by Hercules. Its teeth were sown on the earth to become a crop of armed men.

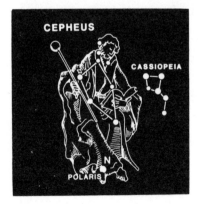

Cassiopeia, Cepheus

From the double star in the Big Dipper's handle, draw a line through Polaris. There, bend the line slightly to the right and keep going the same distance as from the pointers. You'll be in the middle of a 5-star "W" shaped constellation, Cassiopeia. Cassiopeia was the Queen of Ethiopia until she offended the sea nymphs, who bound her to this seat in the sky. The same 5 stars looked to the early Arabs like a giant hand, each one marking a fingertip.

Between Cassiopeia and Draco's head (the 4-star rectangle), you'll find the constellation Cepheus. It's not as bright as Cassiopeia nor the Big Dipper. The Greeks saw it as the "sky father" husband of Cassiopeia. It looks somewhat like a large, A-frame tent, pointing toward Polaris.

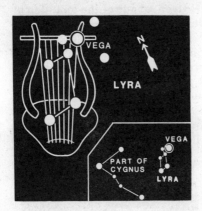 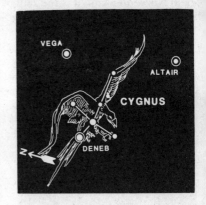

Lyra, Cyngnus (Swan), Hercules

A line from Polaris through the brightest star in the head of Draco points to Vega. Vega is one of the brightest stars in the sky, only 26 light years distant, and part of the 5-star constellation Lyra, the lyre or harp. It's said that this harp was invented by Hermes and given to his half-brother Apollo. The Arabs thought of the same constellation as a swooping Stone Eagle of the Desert, with half-closed wings tucked as it dove for a kill.

A line from Polaris through the brightest star of Cepheus (skirting the back of Cepheus's throne), goes to the star Deneb, the tail of the giant swan Cygnus. Cygnus is a large cross in the sky, with 4 bright stars long and 3 wide. It was known in Arabia as a giant bird called a "Roc" made famous by its conflicts with Sinbad the Sailor. Find the Milky Way stretching across the sky; Cygnus is in full flight along it.

Finally, a line from Polaris skirting west of Draco's head takes you to Hercules. A 4-star rectangle forms his body, with different numbers of stars for his arms, legs and weapons. The rectangle is the key to finding Hercules, but none of its stars are exceptionally bright. It's sometimes hard to find. It's usually nearly straight overhead on summer evenings. Moving from east to west, Cygnus, Lyra and Hercules are all about the same distance from the North Star.

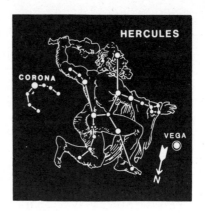

Bootes (Herdsman), Corona Borealis (Northern Crown)

Follow the curve of the Big Dipper's handle away from the bowl. It leads to another very bright star, Arcturus. Stretching toward the North Star from Arcturus, in the shape of a kite or ice cream cone, is the constellation Bootes, the Herdsman. The kite shape is the body; the 2 legs meet at Arcturus. The Arabs called him the Shepherd, with the idea that the stars around the North Pole resembled a flock of sheep, and he was always going in circles to herd them. He has also been seen as a hunter in pursuit of Ursa Major, the Great Bear.

Between Bootes and Hercules, about the same distance from Polaris, is a 7-star half-circle. This is the Corona Borealis, or Northern Crown. (A similar one lies in the southern sky near the South Pole.) To the Shawnee Indians, these 7 stars were the Celestial Sisters, the fairest (brightest) of them the wife of the hunter White Hawk, Arcturus.

Aquila (Eagle), Delphinus (Dolphin), Ophiuchus (Serpent Holder), Serpens (Serpent)

A line from Polaris through the head of Cygnus the Swan leads to Altair, the bright head of the eagle, Aquila. Altair is only 16 light years away, bright enough to be seen even through city smog. Aquila, the Eagle, is about the same size as Cygnus, and it's easy to imagine Aquila chasing Cygnus along the Milky Way, always a little behind and to the east of its prey.

The Koreans saw Altair and its 2 bright neighbors not as the head and shoulders of an eagle, but as a prince and his servants, banished across the Milky Way by an irate father-in-law. The Prince's bride is our Lyra. Only once a year, on the seventh day of the seventh moon, could the 2 lovers meet by crossing a bridge of magpies over the Milky Way.

Just northeast of the eagle is Delphinus, the 5-star dolphin. It's a small constellation on the edge of the Milky Way, on a direct line from Polaris through Deneb, the tail of Cygnus (Swan).

A large area of the sky south of Hercules is taken up by a vague constellation, Ophiuchus (Serpent Holder) and his 2 serpents, Serpens Caput and Serpens Cauda. The head of Serpens Caput is a bright triangle just south of the Corona Borealis (Northern Crown). The rest of the serpent stretches south, then east towards the Milky Way. The key to this constellation is figuring out what it is not: once you find Hercules and Corona Borealis to the north and Scorpio to the south, you can find Ophiuchus with his 2 serpents in between.

In Greek legend, Ophiuchus was the ship's surgeon for Jason and the Argonauts. He became so skilled that he could restore the dead to life. This caused Pluto to fear for his kingdom of the dead and Ophiuchus was struck with a thunderbolt by Jove and placed among the constellations.

 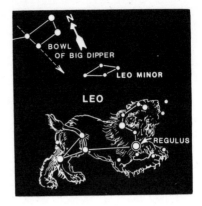

Virgo (Virgin), Leo (Lion)

Remember the pointer stars of the Big Dipper? If you point in the opposite direction from Polaris, past the bottom of the dipper, you come to the bright star Regulus, chest of Leo (Lion). The Lion's mane looks like a backwards question mark running east and then north from Regulus; a triangle of stars to the southeast represents the lion's back legs and tail. The Greeks called it the Nemean Lion, placed in the heavens at the same time as Hercules, the lion's slayer.

Virgo is a dim constellation, difficult to find. Start with the Big Dipper's handle and follow it through Arcturus at the base of Bootes. The next bright star on that arc is Spica in the constellation Virgo. The constellation itself is shaped like a distorted Y, with Spica representing an ear of wheat in the maiden's left hand.

Pegasus, Andromeda

A line from Polaris passing just east of Cassiopeia goes to a large bright square of stars. The star in the northwest corner of the square is part of a small bright triangle. This is Pegasus, the horse; the square represents the horse's body; the triangle is the horse's rear legs. Pegasus is always near the horizon, "upside down" with its head away from Polaris. In Greek mythology, Pegasus sprang from the blood of Medusa after she was slain by Perseus. Later, Bellerophon attempted to ride Pegasus to heaven, but Jupiter, incensed by such boldness, caused an insect to sting the horse. Pegasus threw his rider and then

 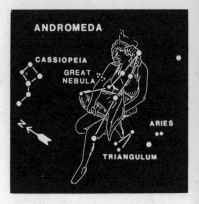

rose alone to his permanent place among the stars.

The bright triangle of stars at one corner of Pegasus is also the end of the constellation Andromeda, the Woman Chained. Alpheratz, the brightest star in the "Great Square" of Pegasus, is the last star in Andromeda. It's the meeting point for 2 lines of stars (4 stars in each line) that represent Andromeda, the daughter of Cepheus and Cassiopeia, chained in exposure to the sea monsters as punishment for Cassiopeia's boasts of her own beauty.

Sagittarius (Archer), Scorpio (Scorpion), Libra (Scales)

These 3 Zodiac constellations are usually close to the southern horizon. Sometimes you can't see them at all; sometimes you see only their northernmost stars. Remember that if Polaris is the head, the Zodiac ring of constellations is a giant belt around the waist of the sky. As Earth tilts during seasonal changes and Polaris moves closer to the northern horizon, this ring moves up from the southern horizon. During the winter months, with Polaris higher in the sky, these constellations move below the horizon and cannot be seen.

Scorpio is the most spectacular. A line from Polaris through the Corona Borealis (Northern Crown) and on through the serpent's head on Ophiuchus passes through 3 very bright stars near the southern horizon. This is the head and the 2 claws of the scorpion. The rest of the scorpion's body winds south, through Antares, a bright star, and continues to a curlique tail. Legend has it that this scorpion killed Orion, the hunter. They were placed in the sky so that Orion, still fearful,

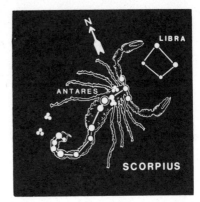

sinks below the northern horizon as Scorpio rises in the south. Antares, the heart of the scorpion, was known to the Chinese as the Fire Star.

Sagittarius (Archer) follows Scorpio across the sky. Four stars represent a bow and arrow; another 5 are the archer's body. The arrow points towards Scorpio. Ancient Arabs saw this constellation as 2 sets of ostriches, passing to and from the celestial river of the Milky Way.

The 4 stars of Libra (Scales) lie between Scorpio and Virgo, in a roughly rectangular shape. The Greeks considered these stars the claws of Scorpio; later they became known as separate constellations.

Perseus (Winged Fighter), Auriga (Charioteer)

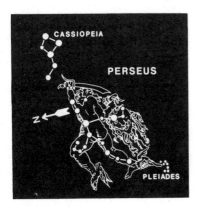

Follow the Milky Way from Cygnus through Cassiopeia. The next constellation is Perseus, a warrior wearing winged sandals. He is holding the head of Medusa in his hand, which he later used to rescue Andromeda from the sea monsters. Perses, the son of Perseus and Andromeda, gave Persia its name. Algol, a bright star in Perseus, was called the "Demon's Head" by the Arabs.

Continuing along the Milky Way, from Cassiopeia through Perseus, you'll come to Auriga (Charioteer). It contains 7 stars in a rough circle, including Capella, called the Goat Star in ancient Greece and the Shepherd's Star in Peru.

Taurus (Bull), Gemini (Twins), Cancer (Crab)

Follow the last three stars in Perseus away from Polaris and you find 7 twinkling stars in a very small cluster. These are the Seven Sisters, the Pleiades (pronounced "Plee-a-dees"). They are also the shoulder of the bull, Taurus. The head of the bull is a bright star, Aldebaran, in the midst of another cluster, and the bull's horns extend into the Milky Way, nearly to Auriga (Charioteer).

Pleiades were seen by Australian aborigines as young girls playing music to young men dancing (Orion's belt); the Finns called the cluster a little sieve with holes in it. The second cluster next to Aldebaran,

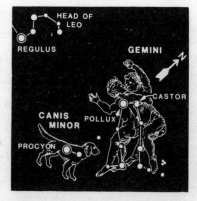

the bull's head, is called Hyades (Hie-a-dees). These were seen by the Greeks as half-sisters to the Pleiades. The whole of Taurus was seen as a bull with huge horns even by ancient South American tribes, and as the jaw of an Ox by natives in the Amazon region.

Gemini (Twins) is a big rectangle. Two stars are inside the Milky Way, just beyond Auriga (Charioteer). The other end of the constellation consists of two bright stars, Castor and Pollux, the twins' heads. To the Phoenicians, the constellation represented 2 gazelles; to the Arabians, 2 peacocks; in India, it was 2 horsemen.

Cancer (Crab) is the most inconspicuous of the Zodiac constellations. Its stars are so dim that it is impossible to see them close to a bright horizon. Cancer lies between Gemini and Leo and is roughly in the shape of an upside-down Y with its tail pointing toward the North Star. Greek myths say it is the crab that was crushed by Hercules in his contest with the Hydra, then raised to the sky by Juno. The Egyptians saw it as a scarab; the Chinese as a quail's head.

Triangulum, Aries (Ram), Pisces (Fishes), Cetus (Whale)

A line from Polaris through the easternmost star in Casseopeia takes you through the end of Andromeda's chain; then through a small 3 star constellation, Triangulum, to one of the 2 bright stars in Aries, the ram. This ram was sacrificed after helping Phrixus escape the wrath of his stepmother, Ino. Its fleece was placed in the Grove of Area, where it turned to gold and became the object of the Argonauts' quest.

Pisces, the fishes, is a huge V-shaped constellation stretching from one leg near Andromeda to a point south of Aries, then back along another long leg toward Aquarius. Most of the stars in Pisces are dim; star finders are vague about its shape since it is usually "falling off" the edge of the map and badly distorted. It rarely comes above the horizon and what parts of it do are usually obscured by mountains or trees since it is always so low in the sky. If you can see a fairly straight line of stars south of Pegasus, you've found half of Pisces.

Cetus, as large as Pisces and lower in the sky, is also rarely seen in the Northern Hemisphere. This is another huge, rambling constellation. The 4 stars in Cetus' head are just south of Aries. It represents a whale or sea monster, fabled to be the monster sent to devour chained Andromeda, but turned to stone at the sight of Medusa's head in the hand of Perseus.

Aquarius (Waterbearer), Equuleus (Colt), Capricorn (Goat)

Follow the triangle of Pegasus (his rear legs) through his tail to the south, and you come to Aquarius (Waterbearer). The sun tends to be in Aquarius during the rainy season, hence the relationship with water. In Babylon, the constellation was an overflowing water jar; in ancient Arabia, a well-bucket; in Rome, a peacock.

Capricorn, between Aquarius and Sagittarius, is generally depicted with the head and body of a goat ending in a fish's tail. It is another one that is tough to make out in the sky. The ancient Hindus called it an antelope; the Chinese considered it a bull.

Equuleus, the colt, is between Delphinus (Dolphin) and Pegasus on the north and Aquarius on the south. It is a small constellation (5 stars) representing the brother of Pegasus.

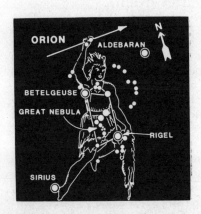 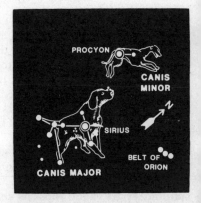

Orion (Hunter), Canis Major (Great Dog)

South of Taurus lies Orion, the hunter. It has 3 bright stars for a belt, 2 more representing a sword. Orion's torso is bounded by two very bright stars, Rigel and Betelgeuse. Orion can be seen from most of Earth, north and south, at one time of the year or other. Mythology holds that he was inflicted with a scorpion sting because of his boastfulness. Then he was placed in the sky in such a way that he could escape whenever his slayer, Scorpio, rose in the east.

Canis Major (Great Dog) is a southern sky constellation, just south-east of Orion. Sirius, its brightest star, lies just on the edge of the Milky Way. From the earliest times, it has been the dog of Orion, shown sitting up and watching his master.

The Hindus knew it as the Deer Slayer, who shot an arrow, which is our belt of Orion. The rest of Orion represented to them a prince, stopped by the arrow from pursuing his daughter, Aldebaran (the bright star in the head of Taurus).

The Great Horned Wyoming Jackalope And Other Do-It-Yourselfers

If you stand on your head, squeeze your eyes real tight, count to 10 and don't pass out or fall asleep, you'll awaken to see the Great Horned Wyoming Jackalope. It's seen especially clearly when reflected in high Rocky Mountain lakes. If you happen to be in Northern California, you might see the Giant Hot Tub, with its pointer stars directing you to a local Zen master. And of course, twinkling through the smog of Southern California comes the Spiraling Red Camaro, complete with sooty black exhaust.

We've picked out everything from grapefruits to beer bottles in the sky, depending on our moods. Rather than getting all strung out making exact identifications, or getting frustrated by not seeing the shapes that the constellations are supposed to be, the important thing is to have fun with the process of discovering the stars. When asked what he liked most about backpacking, a 5-year-old friend of ours replied, "I get to eat lots of cookies and stay up as late as I want." On those nights that *you* stay up late, the stars can be enjoyable and agreeable companions, along with a slow-burning fire and some brandy and hot chocolate.

If you really do get turned on by all of this and want more, see the suggested readings in the "Appendix."

EPILOGUE:

Looking Ahead

Backpacking, like anything else that is complicated and beautiful, is never quite finished. There is always more to learn, about yourself and the wilderness, about technique and enjoyment. There is rarely just one way to do things, which means that both common sense and uncommon sensibilities need to be brought to bear on a problem or a project. If you accept that as a reasonable proposition, you'll remain open to the ideas, suggestions, and experience of others. And you'll tinker and fiddle and improvise until you've got a backpacking trip down to where you want it, rather than the way friends, salesmen, old-timers, experts or books tell you it should be done. It's at such a point that *Backpacking: A Hedonist's Guide* will have served its purpose.

The wilderness is getting smaller, and the number of people heading into it is getting larger. If you want to get a feel for the majesty of the backcountry, you'll have to act fast and with knowledge. The better prepared you are to deal with impassive nature—with its demands and your perception of them—the faster you'll be able to get farther into the wilderness. And if your aim in part is to leave the masses behind, if only for a day or two, then being able to negotiate the backcountry is a useful skill to have.

Solitude is perhaps our most rapidly dwindling personal resource, and its natural habitat is out there in the mountains. In a real sense, then, we are the endangered species. If our capacity to be awed by nature is blunted, if we lose the ability to be modest—to be participants in the wilderness rather than masters of it—we shall be diminished. Backpackers are no more high-minded than anyone else, but the very nature of their work—or rather, their play—requires that they stay attuned to the possibilities inherent in the relationship between an individual and the world beyond roads.

If you are high up on a sun-soaked peak one day, enjoying the view and reflecting on the fact that the hard, off-trail hike ended at the second most beautiful campsite in the world; that the bubble-and-fly bagged a panful of trout; that the bread rose, the souffle scored a hit, and the chocolate cake was the best you ever tasted, write a note about it and stick it in the message cairn. Whoever comes along and reads it will treasure your mood and want to make it their own. And who knows? Maybe even we'll come across it sometime down the line, and then we'll know for sure that our book has accomplished its goal.

APPENDIX

Annotated Reading List

All-Purpose Backpacking Books

Keene, Judy, *Travel Light Handbook*. Contemporary Books, Inc.: Chicago, 1979. The minimalist approach to backpacking. Shows you just how little you need to backpack.

Manning, Harvey, *Backpacking One Step at a Time*. Vintage Books: New York, 1980. Deservedly famous as the best introduction to backpacking in print. Comprehensive, readable, reliable. Unsurpassed on how to judge and buy equipment.

Mitchell, Jim, and Gene Fear, *Fundamentals of Outdoor Enjoyment*. Survival Education Association, 9035 Golden Givens Road, Tacoma, Washington 98445. All the information you'll ever need on the art of survival. Based on the idea that a pound of prevention is worth an ounce of cure. Great illustrations; lots of checklists.

Rethmel, R. C., *Backpacking, 6th Ed.,* revised and updated. Follett Publishing Co.: Chicago, 1979. Exhaustive, encylopedic: more than everything you've ever wanted to know about backpacking. Use it as a reference book.

U.S. Department of Agriculture, *Forest Service Program Aid 1239, Backpacking*. U.S. Government Printing Office, 1981. A 52-page brochure that has just about all the basic information you'll need to get started. Strong on conservation and good sense.

Trail Guides

The High Sierra Hiking Guides. By Wilderness Press, 2440 Bancroft Way, Berkeley, California 94704. A series of 21 expert little guides, each based on one of the quadrangles established by the U.S. Geological Survey. Small and light enough to carry with you. Camping stores will have similar guides to other wilderness areas.

Rethmel, R. C., *Backpacking*. (See above). See below for a list of sources for trail information.

Reading Maps and Compass

Bjorn Kjellstrom, *Be Expert with Map & Compass*. Charles Scribner's Sons: New York, 1976. The author is an expert in "orienteering," and puts you through a practical course in the use of maps and compass.

Equipment

See Catalogues, below. These illustrated shoppers' guides are often accompained by expert technical advice.

Manning, Harvey, *Backpacking One Step at a Time*. (See above).

Rethmel, R. C., *Backpacking*. (See above.)

Food

Angier, Bradford, *Wilderness Cookery*. Stackpole Books: Harrisburg, PA, 1970. Everything from big game and reflector ovens to nuts and berries. There's a whiff of mule trains here, but you'll learn about bannock, nagoonberry, and other exotics.

Kinmont, Vikki, and Claudia Axcell, *Simple Foods for the Pack*. Sierra Club Books: San Francisco, 1976. Very "whole earth" — carob, miso, oats, bulgar. The fare is simple and easy.

Beyer, Bee, *Food Drying at Home*. J. P. Tarcher, Inc.: Los Angeles, 1976. Excellent, easy-to-follow introduction to food drying. Lots of good recipes.

Fishing

Farmer, Charles, *Backpack Fishing*. John Olson Co.: Paramlus, N. J., 1976. Promises more than it delivers, but if you can afford expensive equipment and know how to fish already, it's good on where to go and when.

Stars

Baker, David, and David Hardy, *The Larousse Guide to Astronomy*. Larousse & Co: New York, 1981. Comprehensive. Soft-cover but heavy. Excellent illustrations of the constellations, pp. 72-145, which could be cut out and packed into the mountains.

Chartraud, Mark R., III, *Skyguide, A Field Guide for Amateur Astronomers*. Golden Press: New York, 1982. Another basic introduction, well illustrated. Hardcover and heavy. Golden Press has a smaller, soft-cover book, *Stars,* by Herbert S. Zim and Robert H. Baker (1975), which is more convenient but less comprehensive.

Moore, Patrick, *The Pocket Guide to Astronomy*. Simon & Schuster: New York, 1983. Narrow format makes it excellent for packing. Illustrations not as good as first two books, but adequate.

Philips' *Planisphere*. North Star Imports, P.O. Box 28, Rio Dell, CA 95562. Indispensible rotating disc showing principal stars visible for every hour in the year at 42 degrees N. A compact star map. Comes in two sizes, the smaller of which fits easily into a backpack pouch.

Camping News & Information

The following newsletters and magazines often contain excellent suggestions on where to go, information on local conditions, camping ideas, and advice from experts.

Appalachian Trailway News. Appalachian Trail Conference, Box 236, Harpers Ferry, West Virginia 25425

Backpacker. Ziff-Davis Publishing Co., Consumer Division, One Park Ave., N.Y., NY 10016

California Explorer. 45 Woodside Lane, Mill Valley, CA 94941

Camping Journal. Davis Publications, Inc., 380 Lexington Ave., N.Y., NY 10017

Colorado Outdoors. Division of Wildlife, 6060 Broadway, Denver, Colorado 80216

Eastern Outdoors. Eastern Publishing Corp., 24 Legendary Rd., East Lyme, CN 06333

Field & Stream. CBS Publications, 1515 Broadway, N.Y., NY 10036

Fishing World. Allspfort Publishing Corp., 51 Atlantic Ave., Floral Park, NY 11001

Michigan Sportsman. Sportsman Group Publications, 801 Oregon St., Oshkosh, Wisconsin 54901

Minnesota Sportsman. Box 1902, Minneapolis, Minnesota 55460

Montana Outdoors. Department of Fish, Wildlife and Parks, 1420 E. Sixth, Helena, Montana 59601

Outside. Rolling Stone, 745 Fifth Ave., N.Y., NY 10022

Catalogues

REI Co-op Catalogue, R.E.I. Co-op, P.O. Box 88125, Seattle, Washington 98188

Early Winters, Ltd., 110 Prefontaine Place South, Seattle, Washington 98104

L. L. Bean, Inc., Freeport, Maine 04032

Herter's, Inc. Waseca, Minnesota 56093

Sources For Maps—TOPOGRAPHIC
East of the Mississippi:
U.S. Geological Survey, Washington, D.C. 20242

West of the Mississippi:
U.S. Geological Survey, Federal Center, Denver, Colorado 80225

Canada:
Map Distribution Office, Dept. of Mines and Technical Surveys, Ottawa, Ontario

U.S. Geological Survey maps are increasingly available in camping and backpacking stores.

U.S. FOREST SERVICE:
U.S. Forest Service, Washington, D.C. 20240

Local and regional Forest Service offices are listed in the phone directory under U.S. Department of Agriculture, of which the Forest Service is a branch.

U.S. NATIONAL PARKS:

U.S. National Park Service, U.S. Department of the Interior, Washington, D.C. 20240.

Local and regional National Park offices are listed in the phone directory under U.S. Department of the Interior, of which the National Park Service is a branch.

OTHER:

State or county parks often issue trail maps. Call your state or country Parks and Recreation Departments.

There are a great number of hiking and camping organizations. They can be very helpful to both members and non-members by providing information on trails and camping conditions. Ask for addresses at your local camping supply store, or see R. C. Rethmel, *Backpacking,* p. 218, for a list of major national orgainzations.

Sources For Freeze-Dried Foods

Chuck Wagon Foods, 176 Oak Street, Newton, Massachusetts 02164

Mountain House Foods, P.O. Box 1048, Albany, Oregon 97321

Perma-Pak Foods, 40 East Robert Ave., Salt Lake City, Utah 94115

Rich-Moor Foods, P.O. Box 2728, Van Nuys, California 91404

Wilson & Co., Inc., Chicago, Illinois 60601

R. E. I. Co-op, P.O. Box C-88125, Seattle, Washington 98188

INDEX

ABOUT THE AUTHORS

Rick Greenspan teaches auto mechanics at the Alameda Community College in Alameda, California. He is a co-author of *Fixing Cars, A Peoples Primer* (San Francisco Institute for Automotive Ecology, 120 Anderson Street, San Francisco, CA 94110, 1974), a do-it-yourself guide to the wonders of auto repair.

Hal Kahn is a professor of history at Stanford University and the author of *Monarchy in the Emperor's Eyes* (Harvard University Press, Cambridge, Mass., 1971).

Together they have over a quarter-century of backpacking experience. Their friends know them as discriminating "fressers,"* which accounts for their emphasis on the delights of eating, and as the concocters of some of the most original and delightful backpacking trips ever planned and executed. You could look it up.

* In Yiddish, "to fress" means "to eat like a pig."

ABOUT THE ILLUSTRATOR

Gordy Ohliger is himself an avid backpacker. He lives in a small cabin in the woods of the Sierra Nevada foothills of Northern California. He illustrated the trails, creeks, and equipment in this book mainly with the view from his back porch.

We're Into Islands!
OTHER MOON PUBLICATIONS

Finding Fiji by David Stanley
Fiji, everyone's favorite South Pacific country, is now easily accessible either as a stopover or a whole Pacific experience itself. No visas or vaccinations are required! Enjoy picture-window panoramas as you travel from exciting island resorts where Australians meet Americans halfway, to remote interior valleys where you can backpack from village to village. You'll fall immediately in love with the friendly, exuberant people. *Finding Fiji* covers it all - the amazing variety of land and seascapes, customs and climates, sightseeing attractions, hikes, beaches, and how to board a copra boat to the outer islands. *Finding Fiji* is packed with practical tips, everything you need to know in one portable volume. 127 pages, 78 illustrations, 20 color photos, 3 charts, 26 maps, vocabulary, subject and place name index. US $6.95.

South Pacific Handbook by David Stanley
Here is paradise explored, photographed and mapped—the first original, comprehensive guide to the history, geography, climate, cultures, and customs of the 19 territories in the South Pacific. Experience awesome Bora Bora by rented bicycle; scale Tahiti's second highest peak; experience the splendid isolation of an endless talcum beach in New Caledonia's Loyalty Islands; drink *kava* with villagers in Fiji's rugged interior; backpack through jungles in Vanuatu to meet the "hidden people"; marvel at the gaping limestone chasms of Niue; trek along Bloody Ridge in the Solomons where the Pacific War changed course; hitch rides on cruising yachts; live the life of a beachcomber in Tonga; witness the weaving of a "fine mat" under a Samoan *fale*; go swimming with free sea lions in the Galapagos; dive onto coral gardens thick with brilliant fish; see atoll life unchanged in Tokelau or Tuvalu; dance the exciting Polynesian dances of the Cooks. No other travel book covers such a phenomenal expanse of the earth's surface. 25 color plates, 160 b/w photos, 162 illustrations, 127 island maps, 29 town plans, 17 charts, booklist, glossary, index. 578 pages. US $12.95

Japan Handbook by J.D. Bisignani
Packed with practical money-saving tips on travel, food and accommodation, this book dispels the myth that Japan is 'too expensive' for the budget-minded traveler. The theme throughout is 'do it like the Japanese,' to get the most for your time and money. From Okinawa through the entire island chain to Rishiri Island in the extreme north, *Japan Handbook* is essentially a cultural and anthropological manual on every facet of Japanese life. 520 pages, 92 line illustrations, 29 charts, 112 maps and town plans, 200 photos, 35 color plates, an appendix on the Japanese language, booklist, glossary, index. $12.95.

Indonesia Handbook by Bill Dalton

Not only is Indonesia Handbook the most complete and contemporary guide to Indonesia yet prepared, it is a sensitive analysis and description of one of the world's most fascinating human and geographical environments. It is a travel encyclopedia which scans, island by island, Indonesia's history, ethnology, art forms, geography, flora and fauna - while making clear how the traveler can move around, eat, sleep and generally enjoy his unique travel experience in this loveliest of archipeligos. The London Times called it "one of the best practical guides ever written about any country." 602 pages, 137 illustrations and b/w photos, 123 maps. US$12.95.

Alaska-Yukon Handbook: A Gypsy Guide to the Inside Passage and Beyond by David Stanley

Embark from exciting cities such as Seattle, Vancouver, and Victoria, and sail to Alaska on the legendary Inside Passage. Tour the great wilderness ranges and wildlife parks of the North. Backpack across tundra to snowcapped peaks; stand high above the largest glaciers on earth; run mighty rivers. See nature as it once was everywhere. Travel by regular passenger ferry, bus, and train, or just stick out your thumb and go. Sleep in campgrounds, youth hostels, and small hotels tourists usually miss. Dine in unpretentious local eating places or just toss out your line and pull in a salmon. In addition to thousands of specific tips on Alaska and Yukon, this handbook includes detailed coverage of Washington and British Columbia. *Alaska Yukon Handbook* is the only travel guide which brings this whole spectacular region within reach of everyone. 244 pages, 86 illus., 76 b/w photos, 37 color photos, 70 maps, booklist, glossary, index. US$7.95.

Guide to Catalina Island by Chicki Mallan

Whether they come by yacht, ferry, or airplane, visitors to Santa Catalina will find this the most complete guide to America's most unique island. *Guide to Catalina* provides essential travel information, including complete details on hotels, restaurants, camping facilities, bike and boat rentals, as well as about boat mooring and skin diving, to make it a must for marine enthusiasts. Everyone, however, will benefit from *Guide to Catalina's* other features -historical background, natural history, hiking trail guides, general travel and recreation tips. Maps, charts, 4 color pages, photos, illustrations, index, 142 pages. US$5.95.

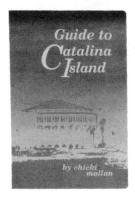

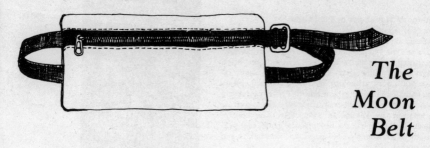

The Moon Belt

A new concept in money belts. Made from highly durable, water repellent polyester cotton blend fabric for maximum all-weather comfort. The 3.75x8 inch pouch is worn around the waist concealed inside your clothes. Many thoughtful features: 1 inch wide nylon webbing, heavy-duty zipper, and 1 inch wide high test plastic slide for easy adjustability. The field-tested Moon Belt comes with extra long webbing; cut your size, then simply seal end with lighted match. Accommodates Traveler Checks, passport, cash. Essential for the traveler. Only $5.95.

ORDER FORM & SHIPPING INFORMATION

QUANTITY	TITLE	1stCLASS or UPS	BOOK RATE	AMOUNT
	ALASKA-YUKON HANDBOOK	$10.95	$9.20	
	BACKPACKING: A HEDONIST'S GUIDE	$9.45	$8.20	
	FINDING FIJI	$9.45	$8.20	
	GUIDE TO CATALINA ISLAND	$8.45	$7.20	
	INDONESIA HANDBOOK	$15.45	$14.20	
	JAPAN HANDBOOK	$15.45	$14.20	
	SOUTH PACIFIC HANDBOOK	$15.45	$14.20	

SUB TOTAL _____

CA SALES TAX (6%) † _____

TOTAL _____

Name _____

Street _____

City _____

State / Province _____ Zip _____ County _____

† *California residents only*   *Make checks payable to:* **MOON PUBLICATIONS**
P.O. Box 1696
Chico, CA 95927 USA

We accept **Visa** and **Mastercharge**

Please send written order with your Visa or Mastercharge

number and expiry date clearly written.

CHECK/MONEY ORDER ENCLOSED FOR $ _____

☐ VISA   ☐ MASTERCHARGE

CARD NO.   BANK NO.

☐☐☐☐☐☐☐☐☐☐☐☐☐☐☐☐ ☐☐☐☐

Signature _____ expiration _____

note: *We give a 5 percent discount for orders of 3 books or more (saves us postage).*

Please allow 4-30 days for Bookrate, 1 week for UPS or 1st class
THANK YOU FOR YOUR ORDER